Sgript Cymru in association with **Soho Theatre Company**
presents

ART AND GUFF

a play in two acts

by **Catherine Tregenna**

First performed in the UK at Soho Theatre and Writers' Centre,
21 Dean Street, London W1 on 7 March 2001, and then at Chapter
in Cardiff on 4 April 2001.

Sgript Cymru Regd. Charity No: 702117
Soho Theatre Company Regd. Charity No: 267234

soho
theatre company

ART AND GUFF
by **Catherine Tregenna**

Art	Richard Harrington
Guff	Roger Evans
Nicky	Ralph Arliss
Sues	Glenna Morrison
Director	Bethan Jones
Designer	Sean Crowley
Lighting Designer	Elanor Higgins
Casting Director	Gary Howe
Stage Management	Oli James
	Elanor Higgins
Design Assistant	Rhiannon Matthews
Sound Designer	Diane Prentice
Scenic Artist	Tony Gage
Set Construction	J. C. Reilly
Poster Design	Elfen
Photography	Ffotofictions
Press	PS Media

Acknowledgements:

Thanks to Iestyn Jones, Chris Durnall, Clare Isaac and Steve Fisher for their contribution to the initial reading of this play at Dempseys in Cardiff. Thanks also to Jams Thomas, Simon Armstrong and Liz Armon Lloyd for their role in Sgript Cymru's development workshops and Catherine would like to thank Gareth Morris and Jon Tregenna for all their support and help.

Catherine Tregenna, writer

photograph © Brian Tarr

Catherine trained at The Welsh College of Music and Drama and has acted on stage and screen in both Welsh and English before turning her hand to writing. She has written several episodes of the highly popular regional drama *Belonging,* currently in its third series for BBC Wales and has recently finished writing a new ten part drama series set in the Magistrates Court of a small Welsh town, which goes into production in April. *Art and Guff* is her first theatre play and she is delighted that Sgript Cymru and Soho Theatre Company have come together to bring it to the stage.

Bethan Jones, director

Following ten years as a performer in theatre, television and radio, where her work ranged from classical to contemporary drama, from physical theatre to sitcoms and soaps, Bethan became a founding member and Artistic Director of the Welsh language company, Dalier Sylw, which commissioned and produced contemporary plays as well as new adaptations of classical texts. The company also looked to develop ways of working with different languages and produced bilingual and multilingual work. Bethan first began directing with Moving Being in 1990 and has recently begun directing television drama for S4C and BBC Cymru/Wales. Bethan is currently Artistic Director of Sgript Cymru – Contemporary Drama Wales, founded in May 2000, and directed the company's first production *Yr Hen Blant* by Meic Povey, which toured Wales.

Richard Harrington, Art

A member of the National Youth Theatre of Great Britain, Richard was kicked out of school, but not before he played the lead role of *Dafydd* in a film for the BBC, which won him a Best Actor award at BAFTA Cymru. Since then, he has gone on to appear extensively in film and television, in both Welsh and English. His roles include appearances in *Leaving Lenin* (Gaucho Films), *House of America* (September Films), *Streetlife, Oliver's Travels, Tiger Bay, Score* and *Care* (BBC Wales), *Coronation Street* (Granada), *31/12/99* (Bracan/S4C), and *Fondue, Sex and Dinosaurs* (HTV). His theatre work includes leading roles in *Gas Station Angel* (Royal Court Theatre), *Unprotected Sex* (Sherman Theatre), *House of America* (Fiction Factory tour), *Un Nos Ar Faes Peryddon* (Spectacle Theatre) and *Nothing to Pay* (Thin Language Theatre Co.). His radio work includes *Station Road* and *Night Must Fall*.

Roger Evans, Guff

Roger trained at The Guildhall School of Music and Drama. His most recent theatre appearance was in *Everything Must Go* (Sherman Theatre). However, Roger is a familiar face in television for his role as Lip Thomas in the soap *Nuts and Bolts 1&2* (HTV) Roger's film work includes both *Human Traffic* (Fruit Salad) and the soon to be released *Happy Now* (Ruby Films). Other theatre includes *Gas Station Angel* (Royal Court). His television credits also include *The Bill* (Thames), *A Mind to Kill* (HTV), *Wonderful You* (ITV) *Suckerfish* (BBC Wales) and *Syth* (S4C). He is also a regular in the BBC Wales radio serial *Station Road*.

Ralph Arliss, Nicky

Ralph trained at The Drama Centre in London, afterwards working for Charles Marowitz and Thelma Holt at the Open Space Theatre. His career has covered film, television and theatre, playing leading roles for television in *The Lost Tribe, Retrace, Jewel in the Crown* and *Prime Suspect*. His most recent work includes the feature film *Two Days, Nine Lives,* which is awaiting release, and *A Strange Certainty,* a stage play, which formed part of The Rudolf Steiner festival and played at his theatre in Dornach. Ralph has his own film company, developing Cornish drama, and lives in the country near Salisbury.

Glenna Morrison, Sues

Glenna trained at East 15 Acting School. Her theatre credits include *Trainspotting* (on its national and Australian tour), Juliet in *Romeo and Juliet* and Lady Macbeth in *Macbeth* for Incognito. She has also played the title role in *Miss Julie* at the Hawth Studio and Mary Warren in *The Crucible* at Leicester Haymarket, as well as recently participating in development workshops with Suspect Culture. Her television credits include *Taggart, Dangerfield, All at Sea, Buddha's Legs, Pirates* and *Treasure Islands* and she has appeared in pop videos on MTV with cult bands Arab Strap, Galliano and Velocette. Her film credits include *No Such Thing, What Do You Mean We?* and *Fixated.*

Sean Crowley, designer

Since graduating from Wimbledon School of Art in 1985 with a First Class Honours Degree, Sean has worked across the design spectrum in film, opera, theatre and television. Beginning as an assistant to many of Europe's leading designers, his early designs for theatre ranged from one man cabaret to a cast of three hundred in community opera, including *The Miracle Plays* (Cardiff), *Hamlet* (Danish Royal Opera) and *Gaslight* at Hornchurch. Returning to Wales to live in 1993, his work has subsequently included designs for *Cat on a Hot Tin Roof, Duet for One, The Rise and Fall of Little Voice, Pied Piper, The Amazing Mr. Toad, The Emperor's New Clothes, The Importance of Being Earnest, Hansel and Gretel, Dancing at Lughnasa, Neville's Island, Abigail's Party, Alladin, Blue Remembered Hills* and *Pinocchio* (Torch Theatre), *Lludw'r Garreg, New South Wales, Blue Heron in the Womb* and *Pacific* (Theatr Y Byd), *Copper Kingdom* (Grand Theatre, Swansea) and *A Child's Christmas in Wales* (Grand Theatre/Theatre na n'Og), *As You Like It, Learning the Language, A Slag's Gig, The Secret Seven Save The World, Horrible Histories, Pulling The Wool, Christmas Crackers* (Sherman Theatre) and *Flesh and Blood* (Sherman Theatre/Hampstead Theatre) Sean has worked closely with Bethan Jones on *Tair, Y Groesfford, Mayosata, Y Cinio* and *Radio Cymru* for Dalier Sylw and recently on *Yr Hen Blant* for Sgript Cymru. In September 1998, Sean became a full-time lecturer in Theatre Design at The Welsh College of Music and Drama and, since 1999, has been its Head of Design.

Elanor Higgins, lighting designer

Elanor is a graduate of The Welsh College of Music and Drama, where she is now a part-time lecturer in lighting design. Recent lighting designs for Sgript Cymru, as well as Dalier Sylw, includes *Yr Hen Blant, Radio Cymru, Perthyn* and *Wyneb yn Wyneb, Y Madogwys* and *Tair.* She has designed the lighting for *Faust – A Love Story* (National Youth Theatre of Wales), *Rats, Buckets and Bombs* (Nottingham Playhouse), *Cavalleria Rusticana* and *I Pagliacci* (Jigsaw Opera), and *Linda Di Chamounix* (Opera Omnibus). Elanor has worked as a full-time lighting technician for The Welsh National Opera, The Royal National Theatre and The Leicester Haymarket.

sgriptcymru
contemporary drama wales

Formed in May 2000, Sgript Cymru is the national new writing company for Wales, working in both Welsh and English.

"A Welsh theatre is necessary to reveal us to ourselves"

Harri Webb

For the first time, Wales has a company that takes it as its mission to discover, develop and produce the best work of all contemporary Welsh or Wales-based playwrights. It aims to present theatre that is exciting, passionate, fresh and distinctive, to audiences at home and beyond, through a commitment to writer-centred performance of a high standard.

Sgript Cymru emerged out of the successful Welsh language company, Dalier Sylw, under the leadership of Artistic Director, Bethan Jones, which enjoyed ten years of championing a fresh generation of Welsh language playwrights, such as Gareth Miles, Sion Eirian, Geraint Lewis and Meic Povey, to audiences throughout Wales. Now Sgript Cymru has incorporated Associate Director, Simon Harris, who brings his extensive experience to the company, after successes as a freelance writer and director with *Badfinger* and *Nothing to Pay* for his company Thin Language.

As part of its core activity, Sgript Cymru commissions new plays both in Welsh and in English; regularly hosts a development forum for new work called *Sgript Xplosure!* showcasing the work of dozens of new voices; presents its own productions, such as *Yr Hen Blant* by Meic Povey and *Art and Guff* by Cath Tregenna; and works in partnership with other new writing companies, such as Paines Plough, in the co-production of *Crazy Gary's Mobile Disco* by award-winning playwright Gary Owen, as well as, The Traverse Theatre on *Traversing The Globe* and Soho Theatre and Writers' Centre.

In addition, the company offers support to writer development from the grassroots level - through schemes such as our vibrant Young Writers Group and community access through our Community Writer initiative – to individual contact with our Literary Department.

"providing an invaluable resource to writers in Wales"

www.theatre-wales.co.uk

Sgript Cymru is committed to producing high-quality new plays that bring to light the best theatre writing that Wales can offer and revealing it to audiences in Wales and beyond.

Sgript Cymru

● soho
● theatre company

Soho Theatre and Writers' Centre
21 Dean Street, London W1D 3NE
Admin: 020 7287 5060 Fax: 020 7287 5061
Box Office: 020 7478 0100 minicom: 020 7478 0136
www.sohotheatre.com   email: mail@sohotheatre.com

Bars and Restaurant   *Gordon's*

The main theatre bar is located in Café Lazeez Brasserie on the Ground Floor. The Gordon's® Terrace serves Gordon's® Gin and Tonic and a range of soft drinks and wine. Reservations for the Café Lazeez restaurant can be made on 020 7434 9393.

Free Mailing List: Join our mailing list by contacting the Box Office on 020 7478 0100 or email us at mail@sohotheatre.com for regular online information.

Hiring the theatre: Soho theatre has a range of rooms and spaces for hire. Please contact the theatre managers on 020 7287 5060 or email hires@sohotheatre.com for further details.

Soho Theatre Company

Artistic Director: Abigail Morris
Assistant to Artistic Director: Samantha Potter (temporary)
Administrative Producer: Mark Godfrey
Assistant to Administrative Producer: Tim Whitehead
Literary Manager: Paul Sirett
Literary Officer: Jo Ingham
Associate Directors: Jonathan Lloyd, Mark Brickman
Director of Writers' Programme: Lin Coghlan (part-time)
Director of Young Writers' Programme: Lisa Goldman (part-time)
Development Director: Carole Winter
Acting Development Officer: Elizabeth Freestone
Marketing Manager: Louise Chantal
Press Officer: Angela Dias (020 7478 0142)
Theatre Manager: Catherine Thornborrow
Deputy Theatre Manager: Anne Mosley
Financial Controller: Kevin Dunn
Accounts: Elva Tehan
Duty Manager: James Neville (part-time)
Box Office Supervisor: Kate Truefitt
Box Office/Receptionists: Matt Podmore, Leah Read
Ushers: Tony Boswell, Morag Brownlie, Ryan Clifford, Sharon Degen, Claire Derouesne, Megan Fisher, Claire Fowler, Mary Green, Matthew Hurt, Kristina Moller-Tsakonas, Sam Laydon, Claire Townend and Kellie Wilson.
Production Manager: Nick Ferguson
Chief Technician: Nick Blount
Deputy Chief Technician: Jonathan Rouse
Board: David Aukin *chair*, Cllr Robert Davis *vice chair*, Lisa Bryer, Tony Elliott, Barbara Follett MP, Bruce Hyman, Lynne Kirwin, David Pelham, Philippe Sands, Eric H. Senat, Meera Syal, Richard Wilson OBE, Roger Wingate
Honorary Patrons: Bob Hoskins *president*, Peter Brook CBE, Simon Callow, Sir Richard Eyre

THE SOHO THEATRE DEVELOPMENT CAMPAIGN

Soho Theatre Company receives core funding from Westminster City Council and London Arts but in order to provide as diverse a programme as possible and expand our audience development and outreach work, we rely upon additional support. Many projects are only made possible by donations from trusts, foundations and individuals and corporate involvement.

stone
Gordon's
Bloomberg
TBWA\GGT DIRECT
A&B
Arts & Business

All our major sponsors share a common commitment to developing new areas of activity with the arts. We specifically encourage a creative partnership between Soho Theatre Company, the sponsors and their employees.

This translates into special ticket offers, creative writing workshops, innovative PR campaigns and hospitality events.

The **New Voices** annual membership scheme is for people who care about new writing and the future of theatre. There are various levels to suit all – for further information, please visit our website at: **www.sohotheatre.com/newvoices**

Our new **Studio Seats** campaign is to raise money and support for the vital and unique work that goes on behind the scenes at Soho Theatre. Alongside reading and assessing over 2000 scripts a year, we also work intensively with writers through workshops, showcases, writers' discussion nights and rehearsed readings. For only £300 you can take a seat in the Education and Development Studio to support this crucial work.

If you would like to help, or have any questions, please contact the development department on 020 7287 5060 or at: **development@sohotheatre.com**

We are grateful to all of our sponsors and donors for their support and commitment.

LONDON ARTS   SUPPORTED BY
                     CITY OF
                     WESTMINSTER

PROGRAMME SUPPORTERS

First published in 2001 by Oberon Books Ltd.
(incorporating Absolute Classics)
521 Caledonian Road, London N7 9RH
Tel: 020 7607 3637 / Fax: 020 7607 3629

e-mail: oberon.books@btinternet.com

Cover design: E L F E N

Series design: Richard Doust

Printed in Great Britain by Antony Rowe Ltd, Reading.

Characters

ART

GUFF

NICKY

SUES

The action takes place in a London Flat and a West End pub.

ACT ONE

Scene 1

A large room upstairs in a large house – ART and GUFF's flat. A camp bed is situated to one side. The room consists of a small kitchen area, which is separated from the living area. The couch in the living area has a blanket and pillow on it. On a chest of drawers stands a new, expensive-looking hi-fi and a small pile of CDs. By the side of the camp bed, there is an upturned crate on which are placed a small pile of scripts and a broken lamp stand. From the crate to a cardboard box is a home-made shelf on which stands a row of ART's books. There's a stool by the curtain-less window. A grubby mirror hangs by the flat door. Another door leading off to the bathroom is ajar at the back of the room.

It is 2.30 a.m. The room is barely lit. A key struggles in the lock. After some time the door falls open. ART (mid thirties, tall with drunken, hungry eyes wearing jeans, a white shirt and a long black coat) stumbles in. For a moment behind him we see GUFF (mid-thirties, shorter, heavier build wearing joggers, a stripey tee-shirt and a black suit jacket) about to follow in as the door slams shut in his face.

ART heads for the bathroom.

ART: Turn the light on, wuss. Guff?

> *He goes into the bathroom. There is a knock on the flat door. He calls out.*

> At this time of night!! Guff oh, get the door.

> *The knocking persists.*

> Guff? Get the bastard door, wuss. *Guff?*

GUFF: (*Off.*) Art oh, let me in for fuck's sakes.

> *ART comes out of the bathroom and opens the door.*

> Donkey!

ART: Who came in with me then?

GUFF: You nearly 'ad my nose off, mun.

ART: I could 'ave sworn…

GUFF: I've noticed that about you, wuss. You never hold the door open or nothin'. Ego that is, see. And bad manners.

GUFF looks in the mirror as ART returns to the bathroom.

Christ, I look more like my old man every day.

ART: (*Off.*) Good night though, wuss!

GUFF: Crackin', dog's bollocks.

ART: (*Off.*) I'm on a high see, me. High on life.

GUFF: Life and nine pints of Stella, innit?

ART: (*Off.*) Aye, drunk myself sober though see.

The toilet flushes. ART emerges as GUFF tries to take off his jacket.

Hey, that club was alright.

GUFF: Aye, bit loud though, wuss.

ART: See me dancin' tonight? Smooth I was. King of the Floor, me.

ART picks up the remote control and flicks on the hi-fi. A 'Reef' CD – 'Place Your Hands' plays loudly.

Dance with me, wuss, I've got dancin' feet.

He grabs GUFF's jacket sleeve. The jacket falls to the floor, small change scatters everywhere. GUFF attempts to retrieve his coins.

GUFF: Fuckin' hell, Art.

ART: You said you 'ad no change for a cab. 'Pants on fire', Garfield Jones.

GUFF: I'm a bit peckish, wuss.

ART: How come you never dance then?

GUFF: Stupid, mun. People jiggin' about in a little space.

ART: You used to in School discos. I remember. Like this.

ART takes awkward steps side to side, knocking each foot against his ankle in a slow rhythm – a laboured simpleton impression.

Kicking yourself in the shins, mun. You must have been black and blue for days after.

Pause.

Why did you dance like that, then?

GUFF: Bugger off.

ART: Step, kick, step, kick.

GUFF: How about you tonight then? I don't think John Travolta'll be losin' any sleep over your moves, wuss. King of the Floor, my eye. Like a bastard windmill you were. You hit a woman in the face twice.

ART: Oh aye. Step, kick…step, kick.

GUFF: Well, at least I only injure myself, innit?

The two face each other doing exaggerated impersonations of each other's dance styles. GUFF twists his arms wildly and shuffles his feet. ART steps and kicks. GUFF stops.

Aye, aye.

ART: Step, kick, step, kick…

GUFF: Aye, stop it now, wuss. It's/

ART/GUFF: (*Together.*) /childish, mun.

GUFF stares at ART.

Cut it out. *Cut it out, mun!*

ART: You hate it when I do that, don't you?

GUFF: You…hate…it…don't you?

GUFF can't pull it off.

ART: Look at you there trying to do it!

ART collapses into uncontrollable laughter, hands on his knees.

The laughter turns into a racking cough. GUFF rises, goes into the kitchen area and pours a glass of water. ART holds out his hand. GUFF returns, drinks it down.

Aye, cheers, wuss.

GUFF: Self-inflicted, innit? Smokin', mun. Cancer sticks. Don't get it, see. Never will. You're like a barrel of gravel, wuss. Never felt the need myself, see.

ART: Smug bugger.

ART lights a cigarette. GUFF waves away the smoke.

GUFF: Don't want to sleep in it, mun.

ART turns the volume up on the hi-fi with the remote.

ART: Don't hit me, wuss.

GUFF: Give me that! Give! It's my fuckin' hi-fi so fuckin' hand it over, right?

They wrestle. ART, laughing, holds the remote out of GUFF's reach.

Give!

ART: Alright, alright, don't get so proprietorial, mun!

ART lets GUFF have it. GUFF switches the hi-fi off and sits with the remote in his lap.

You're so easy to wind up, aye.

GUFF: And you're a pain in the fuckin' arse.

ART: I know. I'm sorry.

GUFF: Infant!

ART: Weeble!

GUFF: Twat!

ART: Here endeth *that* Battle of Wits.

Pause.

Hey, that bloke in the Crown. He was a few butties short of a picnic, aye.

GUFF: Thick as shit, mun.

Pause.

I can't believe you sold him your return ticket though.

ART: (*Cod Humphrey Bogart accent.*) Sweetest twenty bucks a monkey ever made.

GUFF: You can't go home now though.

ART: Couldn't anyway. It expired last week.

GUFF: Christ, mun. I should have sold him mine an' all.

ART: One man makes but one journey, wuss.

GUFF: Why the fuck did he want to go to Kidwelly, anyhow?

ART: a) He's never been. b) It's got a castle and c) He's got sod all else to do.

Pause.

Oh yeah…and I told him Julie Christie lived there and drank in the White Horse on Wednesdays.

GUFF: (*Contemplating the man's imminent disappointment.*) Shit.

ART: And the beauty of it is he'll never find out I lied cos the bastard ticket's expired! Genius, mun.

GUFF: The words 'sand' and 'Arab' spring to mind.

ART: You want to watch that.

GUFF: Toast?

ART: To who?

GUFF: Toast mun. D'you want some?

ART: No, can't be bothered.

GUFF: That's so true…munch, munch innit?

Pause.

I'm hungry though.

ART: Well, have some toast then.

GUFF: I'm tryin' to lose weight, though. I'm fat, see, well, well-covered innit. You smoke see, keeps you thin.

ART: And rots my lungs.

GUFF: Haven't eaten since lunch see, apart from that kebab.

ART: Have some toast, Guff.

GUFF: Shouldn't, though.

ART: Tell you what. Pretend you've just had some, then. See if that works.

GUFF: How d'you mean?

ART: Mind over matter, wuss. Think to yourself, 'I've just eaten a whole plate of hot buttered toast, and now I'm full'.

GUFF: You've just made me more hungry now, saying that.

ART: Just try it, mun. My sister used to do it with chocolate bars.

GUFF focuses, concentrating.

GUFF: No, that's daft, mun. I can't imagine I'm full, can I?

ART: My sister could.

GUFF: Aye well, she's a woman, wuss. It's all psychological with them, innit, food? It's like a hole in my gut, see.

ART: (*Slowly.*) Have some toast, then.

GUFF: Don't you want anything, then?

ART: Guff, me eating won't make you less fat.

GUFF: I get headaches, see, my blood sugar levels go all to cock/

ART: /*Jesus, Are we goin' to discuss this for the rest of our bastard lives?*

GUFF: Alright, alright. You should try wearing a Fat-suit, wuss. Then you'd be more sympathetic, aye.

He goes into the kitchen.

No bread 'ere, mun. Look at us, no bread. How old are we?

He opens the fridge door, drinks the remains of a pint of milk.

Starvin' now, see.

ART: That mirror over there by the door's a good one see. Makes you look thinner at certain angles.

GUFF: Does it? I thought maybe I'd lost a few pounds.

ART: Trouble is, you can't look in any other mirrors, then. Cos it's a letdown.

GUFF: I don't know. Wherever I look it's me I see.

21

ART: Aye but which me innit?

Pause.

Hey, we have good chats, wuss.

GUFF: We have good chats cos you don't listen, wuss.

ART: Talk, mun.

GUFF: Cheap it is.

ART: Some people are uncomfortable in silences, see.

Silence.

Aye, mun. Nobody knows where we are, mun.

GUFF: Quiet pint, mun. Pissin' it away when you could have been perfectin' your screenplay. The couch for me again, I take it?

GUFF turns out the light and takes off his shoes.

No Guff, you have the bed, wuss. I know you've got a bad fuckin' back.

GUFF lies down on the couch.

ART: I'll get a call tomorrow. I can feel it in my bones. It's reachable see, Guff. It's out there. Those thickoes who can't see it mun, what do they know? Four rejections, their loss I say. Four down, five to go. Can't wait to see their faces back home. Sad old Art writin' away in his little Mobile Library. That's how they see me see, through their little narrow eyes. Well they'll eat their words, hats, teeth – their whole bastard heads when I go back a success, you watch. They can all come to my Premiere/

GUFF: (*Drifting to sleep.*) /Headless.

ART: I can't wait see.

Pause.

Guff, oh!

GUFF: What?

ART: You believe in me, don't you. Cos I believe in you, see. I believe in your poems.

GUFF: You've never read 'em.

ART: London, mun. The great thing about London is you can meet people and never see them again. Great, mun.

GUFF: Sleepin' mun.

ART: I like this see, rambling off to sleep.

Pause.

Forty's my dead-line see. If I don't make it by then, I'll give up, go back and never write a bastard line again. Not one…single…semi-colon. Too secure we've been see. Too much love. Our parents suffering to provide for us, so we could do anything, be anything. It's a curse, mun, a curse full of choices – too many options. Degrees and dreams and what do we do? Fancy ourselves as writers and poets only no-one's pushin' us. And we don't push ourselves cos a Mobile Library and a Hardware store's not so bad and we can always play at bein' philosophers down the pub, innit? This is it now though, Guff. No more playing.

GUFF chuckles, arms folded over his chest. ART sits up.

Aye, it's fun though, innit. Playing.

GUFF chuckles again.

What? What? What mun? Guff? Guff?

GUFF mutters, sound asleep.

I wish you wouldn't do that, wuss.

Pause.

I'll pitch from the rooftops if I have to, see. Guff?

ART lies down on the camp bed. After a while we hear the sound of ART's zip coming down. He lets out a small sigh.

Scene 2

A few days later. The flat is empty and looks somewhat tidier. There's a Top-Man bag on ART's bed. The blanket and pillow case are gone from the couch. The 'Kinks' play on the hi-fi – 'Lazing on a sunny afternoon'.

ART stands, a damp towel round his waist, holding the broken table lamp in his hand.

ART: And furthermore I'd like to thank all those who showed no faith in me, those who spat, pissed and shat on my ideas. I haven't the time, unfortunately, to mention all of you but you know who you are. For without those relentless knocks from those lesser talents, I might never have been forced into directing, producing and starring in 'Sleeping Dog'. Thank you because my degradation became my motivation and that's why I stand here before you, tonight, holding this award. My mother once told me 'Never accept advice from those less successful than you want to be'.

Pause.

Her being assistant manager at the local Spar, this wasn't the easiest advice to take on board, but Mams are in a category of their own and I thank her for her faith in me. I dedicate this award, however, to a man I've never met. Happy viewing Gregory Townsend – this film could have been yours.

A key in the door. ART chucks the lamp stand under the bed, grabs his fags and the Top-Man bag and dashes into the bathroom. GUFF enters, carrying a large holdall, a binbag full of clean clothes and a newspaper. He dumps them on the sofa.

GUFF: Art, oh! Where are you?

ART: (*Off.*) Well, considering there's only two rooms and I'm not in the one you're in, where d'you think I am, Guff?

GUFF: Bathroom is it?

From the bathroom we hear the sound of clapping hands.

Done the laundry anyway.

ART: (*Off.*) Not my silk shirt I hope.

GUFF: No, mun.

GUFF digs into the holdall, locates a crumpled silk shirt and stuffs it deep into ART's drawer. He picks up an open can of Pepsi and swigs.

Art? I phoned home anyway.

ART: (*Off.*) What?

GUFF turns the volume down, goes to the bathroom door.

GUFF: I said I phoned home.

ART: (*Off.*) Everything alright?

GUFF: Fine, great, yeh, yeh…well no actually. I just found out we had a bereavement in the family yesterday.

ART: (*Off.*) No. Who?

GUFF: My Auntie Jo, the one who brought me up, you know. Like a mother to me really, but there you go. Eighty two, see. Good innings. Blessing really…for who I'm not quite sure though.

Pause.

Life goes on, see.

ART: (*Off.*) Sorry wuss.

GUFF: Aye well...

ART: (*Off.*) Your Dad's alright, though?

GUFF: Yeh, fine mun. Apart from the gout. He can't walk, mun. Hey, listen Art. Your mam's after our address. She wants to send you up some woollies.

ART: (*Off.*) It's April!

GUFF: She's worried wuss.

ART: (*Off.*) Hey, I came up here to get away from those woollies. And never was there a greater reason to leave home, Guff, believe you me.

GUFF: I know, wuss. I've seen 'em.

GUFF starts sorting the laundry.

I don't see why they can't know where we are though.

ART: (*Off.*) No way wuss. Are you forgetting last time? They came up to rescue us, mun!

GUFF: Aye but we needed rescuin' though.

ART: (*Off.*) We were twenty bastard four years old mun!

GUFF: Aye with nine days to go till Giro day and only half a pack of Jammy Dodgers to live off. And they were stale.

Pause.

Mind you, I like them soft. Hey, I've got something to tell you an' all. Art oh, what are you doin' in there? You're not wanking again, are you?

ART: (*Off.*) Fuck off! Havin' a shave. No law against it, is there?

The bathroom door opens and ART emerges in a suspiciously new-looking pair of knee-length shorts.

GUFF: Shorts!

ART: (*Pointing defensively at GUFF's legs.*) Longs!

GUFF: Nice Art. New are they?

ART: No, had them ages.

GUFF: Never seen 'em before.

ART: Christ, can't a man put on a pair of shorts without triggering off a national dispute?

ART picks up some dirty mugs and goes to the kitchen, fills the kettle, switches it on.

GUFF: I only said they were nice.

ART: Aye, only with a big 'Doesn't Art Look Stupid!' smile on your face.

GUFF: I didn't expect them, 'at's all.

Pause.

They're alright.

ART: Can we stop talking about them now?

GUFF: Look, if you don't want attention, wear your jeans same as always.

ART: Yeh well, maybe I don't want to put on the same pair of stinking jeans day in day out. I mean I respect your consistency of style, Guff, but for fuck's sake, you'll be buried in your bloody joggers, mun…and those three for the price of two Hypervalue tee-shirts with stripes and egg stains all down their bastard fronts.

GUFF: Nothing wrong with my tee-shirts.

Pause.

Primark, actually. An' they're clean now. Well, apart from this one.

Pause.

I mean, pardon me for sayin' Art, but I'm a poet, wuss, not Jeff Bloody Banks.

ART: And I'm allowed to put on a pair of shorts without being made to feel as if I'm breaking the Kidwelly Boys Abroad Dress Code. Alright?

GUFF: Fair enough.

GUFF resumes sorting the laundry.

ART: Good.

GUFF picks up his clean clothes and puts them in the chest of drawers. ART sits on the stool, by the window and lights a cigarette.

Any mail then?

GUFF: No.

ART: Great.

GUFF: No news is good news.

ART: When? I mean, what the fuck does that mean?

Pause.

No news is, as it says, …no news…no more, no less.

GUFF: My giro didn't come either. Due today, mun. Fuck it. Ring 'em later. Hey, we've got to start thinking more about jobs, wuss.

ART: Jobs. What people do for a living. There, I've started.

GUFF: Aye, most people.

ART: No skills, wuss. You're the manual man.

GUFF: Have to do something soon, anyway. Won't be able to live off my giros once our savin's run out.

ART: Not my fault the bastard Library Service refused to say they'd sacked me, is it?

GUFF picks up his paper.

GUFF: I never said that, did I? Just running a bit short is all.

ART: Unfortunate choice of phrase for one so vertically challenged.

GUFF heads for the bathroom.

GUFF: Aye, quip away, chip away. Too clever for your own bastard good you are.

GUFF goes in, shuts the door.

ART: And yet not clever enough. (*Louder.*) Tea?

ART goes to the kitchen, calls out.

And what's on the agenda today, then?

GUFF: (*Off.*) Breakfast to kick off, is it? I'm starved, mun.

ART: (*With GUFF.*) I'm starved, mun.

GUFF: (*Off.*) I heard that.

ART laughs at the sink as he swills the mugs.

There is a knock on the door. ART stops, stands, puts down a mug very quietly. Another knock. He creeps along to the bathroom door.

(*Off shouting suddenly.*) Are you goin' to get that or what? Art, oh!

ART: Alright, alright.

ART glances in the mirror before opening the door. A tall man with matted hair wearing baggy trousers and a large multi-coloured jumper stands there. He is late fortyish, he looks at ART for a few seconds. ART's voice, when he speaks, seems to lower a register.

Alright?

NICKY: Yeh, listen, we live downstairs yeh, only we've (*He laughs a little.*) um...we've sort of locked ourselves out.

ART: Oh, right.

NICKY: Yeh and we wondered if you might have a bread knife.

Pause.

Or any long knife would do, actually.

Pause.

So we could get in.

ART: Right. I'm, yeh...hang on.

ART goes to the kitchen. NICKY steps into the room followed by SUES. She is slight, pale and Scots with blonde dreadlocks in a pony-tail. She is younger than NICKY – about 29. She wears several layers of dark clothes. ART opens and shuts drawers as they stand in the doorway.

Normally have sliced.. when we've got some in, like. *Guff, oh! Have we got/*

The bathroom door opens. GUFF comes out.

GUFF: (*To NICKY and SUES.*) /Alright?

NICKY: Hi.

ART: They want to borrow a 'knife'.

SUES: We're locked out.

GUFF: Oh, right.

ART: I couldn't find one.

GUFF: Aye, there's one somewhere.

He goes to the same kitchen drawer and pulls out a large rusty bread knife. He hands it to NICKY.

There you go. (*To ART.*) Where were you lookin',
then?

NICKY: Cheers.

GUFF: From downstairs are you?

SUES: That's right.

GUFF: Funny place this, livin' above people you don't
know. Come in, mun.

They step further in. SUES shuts the door.

So, you've met Art?

NICKY: Well…

GUFF: No sense of manners, see. Brought up in a good old
Southwalian workin' class household, me. Always serve
tea in the parlour and always wave Goodbye from the
front doorstep when your guests leave. And on that
note, tea?

NICKY: Yeh, cheers. I'm Nicky by the way and this is Sues.

GUFF: I'm Guff, also known as Garfield and this is/

ART: /Art.

GUFF: Also known as painting, drawing, and…any creative
skill you could think of, really.

ART: Guff's the comedian.

NICKY: So, you must be the straight man, yeh?

GUFF: Oh, I don't know, he likes a dash of lime in his
lager. Hey, sorry mun, don't know what's the matter with
me. Verbal diarrhoea this morning. Sit down, mun.

GUFF goes to the kitchen. ART follows him.

ART: (*Quietly, to GUFF.*) What are you playin' at?

GUFF: (*Loudly.*) What?

> *GUFF opens the fridge.*

No milk, mun. What's new? I'll be back in a sec.

ART: I'll go.

GUFF: No, it's alright.

ART: Let me go, mun.

GUFF: No, I need to phone my Dad back, anyway.

ART: Well, how long are you goin' to be? People want tea.

GUFF: Two secs. Promise.

> *GUFF's out the door. ART waits, then comes into the adjoining room. He lights a cigarette. ART offers the pack to NICKY and SUES.*

NICKY: No, ta. I'll have one of these.

> *NICKY opens a tin of rollies, takes one. ART offers him the lighter.*

Cheers.

> *ART waits. NICKY doesn't return the lighter.*

Lovely day, mate.

ART: Yeh, bit of a park day, innit.

SUES: D'you go to the park?

ART: No.

> *Pause.*

Should do, though.

NICKY: Why?

ART: Don't know, really. Always hear people sayin' they live somewhere and never see the sights.

SUES: Where are you from?

ART: Kidwelly. South West Wales.

NICKY: Oh, I know.

ART: Do you?

NICKY: Been there.

ART: Aye, it's alright. Got a castle. Well, I expect you
noticed that. I've never been to it, mind. (*He Laughs.*)
There you go, see. Lived there for thirty odd years
and…'never seen the sights!'

NICKY: (*Smiling.*) It's quite interesting, actually. If you like
history, that is. I love all that – the links to times past,
treading the same path as kings, heroes, saints. Seeing
what their own eyes saw. I love it, man.

'There is a history in all men's lives
Figuring the nature of the times deceas'd'.

ART: Yeah.

Pause.

What d'you both do then?

SUES: I used to be a trapeze artist but I injured my spine so
now I work with disadvantaged children.

ART: Oh, good. Trapeze…wow…didn't expect that.

NICKY: (*Indicating cigarette.*) Is there an…?

ART: Oh, aye. I'll get one.

ART goes to the kitchen and fetches a saucer for an ashtray.

Are you in the circus business, Nick?

NICKY: Kee!

ART: Sorry?

NICKY: Nick-ee!

SUES: He hates to be called Nick.

SUES goes to look through the books by ART's bed.

ART: Oh, right. Yeh, I hate Arthur an' all.

SUES: Are these your books?

ART: Yes.

NICKY: I'm a lighting technician and sound advisor. But I do a bit of clown-work and juggling from time to time. What about you?

ART: Oh, I'm a writer.

NICKY: Anything published?

ART: No but there's a lot of interest, you know.

Pause.

Beats driving lorries for a living anyhow.

SUES: Is that what you did?

ART: Yeh, yeh.

NICKY: Novels or plays?

ART: Films, really.

NICKY: Keep the faith. I paint from time to time.

ART: D'you sell any?

SUES: That's not why he does it.

NICKY looks to ART and smiles.

NICKY: Label.

ART: Sorry?

NICKY: On your shorts, mate.

ART looks, finds the label, whips it off and tucks it in his pocket.

ART: Thanks.

SUES: D'you like Camus or d'you just keep him on the shelf?

ART: Oh, that, *L'Etranger*. Nostalgic reasons, really. First book I read that I felt I really understood.

NICKY: That's its job.

ART: You're from Scotland, then?

SUES: I am, though my father was French.

ART: Oh, I did French for O level. *Je t'aime!*

Pause.

Sorry, don't know why I said that. Wonder where Guff's got to? Just going to the…

ART goes into the bathroom as GUFF bursts in through the flat door finishing the remains of a pastie and carrying a happy shopper bag.

GUFF: Sorry folks. Got caught up. Right, tea. Where's Art?

SUES: In there.

GUFF: Hidin' is he?

ART comes out immediately.

ART: You took your time.

GUFF: Had to go up the road. 'Open All Hours' was shut.

ART takes the bag and goes to the kitchen. NICKY picks a beer mat off the table, reads it.

ART: (*To GUFF.*) I'll do it.

GUFF: Put the biscuits on a plate then.

NICKY: (*To ART.*) Didn't know you wrote poems as well?

GUFF: Jesus, that's mine, mun.

NICKY: It's nice.

GUFF: It's not finished, really.

ART: (*Calling out.*) Started it six years ago, mind.

SUES: Can I see it?

GUFF: Keeps the wolves from the door of the mind, see.

NICKY: That's right.

GUFF: It's nothin' special. Moments, really. I'm about to start a new one. My Auntie Jo/

ART: /Milk for everyone?

SUES: I won't have any tea.

NICKY: Black for me. One sugar, ta. (*To GUFF.*) Sorry, you were saying?

GUFF: Oh aye, no, well she passed away yesterday, my Auntie Jo, and she was like a mother to me really/

ART: /Brought him up.

GUFF: Eighty two she was, see but I still didn't expect her to go. No-one did. Funeral's Friday. Just been on the phone with 'em now. I'll be one of the bearers, see. Be wierd, mun.

ART: This Friday?

GUFF: Aye. At noon. I said we'd both be there. (*To NICKY and SUES.*) If I manage to finish it, I'd like to read it out. Well it's for her, innit? The poem.

SUES: Did you write her one while she was alive?

GUFF: No.

SUES: Pity.

SUES gives the beer mat back to GUFF. ART hands NICKY and GUFF their tea, offers biscuits round. He takes out a cigarette, goes over to NICKY.

ART: Mind if I…?

NICKY lights the cigarette with ART's lighter, then leaves it on the arm of the chair.

Thanks.

GUFF: So what d'you folks do then?

SUES: I work with kids.

ART: She used to be a trapeze artist.

GUFF: What? Bit of a high-flier were you? (*Guffaws.*) How…what d'you do with kids, like?

SUES: Counselling, mainly. Drug addicts, runaways, potential suicides…

GUFF: Good, mun. Worthwhile that, innit. Aye, aye. And you, Nick?

ART: Kee.

NICKY: Nothin' at the moment. Resting, as it were, between gigs.

GUFF: Oh, musician, is it?

NICKY: Technician.

GUFF: Oh aye, I always fancied that, see. Bein' on the road with a band. Sleepin' on the bus, trashing hotel rooms, coppin' off with groupies… (*Remembers SUES.*) Or not, innit.

NICKY: Gets tedious after a while.

GUFF: Yeh, I could see how it could.

Pause.

Good, good.

SUES: So you're both Great Writers in the making?

GUFF: Oh well, I don't know about that. I suppose so, in a sense. Dreamers we are see, innit Art? Just two dull boys from Kidwelly, really. But we're havin' a go, see. And that's important I think. Cos if all else fails and I 'ave to go back to Kidwelly and work in a bastard Hardware store for the rest of my days, well at least I can say I tried innit/

ART: /Where are you from, Nick-ee?

NICKY: Tiverton.

GUFF: Anyway…

NICKY: (*To GUFF.*) You're right. Nurse those dreams. Tap it, don't stem it.

GUFF: It's not so bad for Art, see. I mean, at least if he goes back to his Mobile Library, he'll be surrounded by books. Even if they're written by some other bastard, innit?

Slight pause.

Aye, lovers of words we are really.

NICKY: (*Re. beer mat.*) Would you sign this for me, mate?

GUFF: What, that beer mat?

NICKY: Yeh, a poem on a beer mat. It's nice. I'd like it. Oh, is this your only copy?

GUFF: No, no. I copy them all down in 'ere.

GUFF takes out poem pad and pen and signs the beer mat.

Hey, my first autograph, mun. I've got some more in here, if you're interested, like.

NICKY: Sure, yeh, some other time. Cheers for this.

NICKY holds up the knife.

And this. Get it back to you, yeh?

GUFF starts to follow them to the door.

SUES: Will you wave us Goodbye from the doorway?

GUFF: No, bit extreme that.

He stops in his tracks. They leave.

ART: Don't ever do that to me again, alright?

GUFF: What?

ART: Leavin' me with those two.

GUFF: They're nice people, mun.

ART: Posers, the pair of them.

GUFF: Been in London too long, that's all.

ART: And then you go and spring that bastard funeral on me.

GUFF: Oh sorry Art, I'll ask them to postpone it, shall I? Till you're ready to deal with it.

Jesus, you're like a big baby sometimes, honest to God.

GUFF takes out his poem pad, sits on the sofa. Silence.

ART: Sorry, wuss.

Pause.

I've just been a bit edgy these last few days. Waiting. No calls, you know. It's frustrating, mun.

GUFF: I know.

Pause.

Hey, maybe *I've* got some news.

Pause.

D'you want to hear it?

ART: You're going to tell me anyway.

GUFF: No skin off my nose if I don't.

GUFF fiddles with a poem.

ART: Tell me your news, wuss.

GUFF: No, you're alright.

ART watches him.

What?

ART: Tell me your news.

GUFF: Why, so you can put the dampeners on it?

ART: Christ mun, just tell me, will you?

GUFF puts down his pad, looks at ART.

GUFF: Oh I don't know, it's had too much of a build-up, now.

ART: Guff! What mun?

GUFF: Well…

ART: This better be good.

GUFF: (*Rising.*) Forget it!

ART: Guff, no mun. Please.

Pause.

Tell me. I'm all ears.

GUFF: No, it's just the woman in the launderette and me got talkin', right? She's lovely actually. Bit rough around the edges but nice all the same. Anyway, turns out she sings part-time in clubs and stuff and is looking for new lyrics. So she wants to see my poems.

ART: Oh. Oh, great mun. Great news.

GUFF: I know.

ART: Tidy. (*Trying.*) Good.

GUFF: *And* she's got a sister.

ART: I'm not interested/

GUFF: / *Who* used to go out with Gregory Townsend. Heard of him?

ART: Well yeh, he's Chief Drama Script Editor for *Carlton*, innhe? I sent him a script, mun. So what then? Can she set up a meeting?

GUFF: Well no, not really. It was all a bit acrimonious apparently. But Kaye says she knows his lunch-time watering hole, like. Her sister used to meet up with him there.

ART: Right.

GUFF: Well, it's a start innit? I mean, you've had bugger all luck getting an appointment with any of them. And for all you know, he's been too busy to read it yet, but if we go along, keep our ears to the ground, then maybe you could get chattin' to him, then you could mention what you do, casual like, and then slip him the script innit? It's/

ART/GUFF: (*Together.*) Worth a bastard try, aye!

ART: Hey, nice one Guff.

He claps his friend a little awkwardly on the back.

41

GUFF: Lookin' out for you see, boy. Shit, we should go. It's nearly twelve now.

ART ducks down in front of the mirror.

Why d'you do that, wuss?

ART: Best angle, mun.

GUFF ducks a little.

See, see how good you look. Hey, you're gettin' a bit of a bald patch there, wuss.

GUFF: I know.

ART grabs his jacket and a script, gets out a cigarette.

ART: 'Sleeping Dog' – great title see.

GUFF: Great script, wuss. A Jury Prize waiting to happen.

ART: Hey, that bastard hippy stole my lighter.

GUFF: Easy mistake to make, see.

GUFF whips off his dirty tee-shirt and pulls on an identical clean one.

ART: That's you ready then, is it?

GUFF: Aye, chop, chop, skates on.

ART: Hang on. Tell me straight, wuss. Do these look stupid?

GUFF: No, mun.

ART: It is a bit chilly though innit?

GUFF: Come on Art. We haven't got time for this.

ART clocks himself in the mirror. Before they leave. The door slams after them. Moments pass. ART bursts back through the door.

ART: Two secs, mun. I promise.

He pulls off his shorts and tugs on his jeans, catching them on his unremoved shoes. He kicks off the shoes in desperation and stumbles back towards the door.

Guff! Guff! Guff. Wait! I don't know where we're bastard goin' mun.

ART is out the door shoes in hand.

Scene 3

A London pub. ART and GUFF enter. A few middle-aged men sit around drinking.

GUFF: C'mon, donkey boy!

ART: Sure this is it?

GUFF: For the third time, yes, wuss. (*To BARMAN.*) Two pints of Heineken please, mate, one with a dash of lime.

ART: Shit, what'll I say, mun?

GUFF: Look, calm down wuss. Let's see if he comes in first.

ART: What time is it?

GUFF: Lunch-time, alright?

ART: You better tell us what he looks like. He could be here now for all we know.

GUFF: I can do better than that, mun.

He reaches into his pocket and pulls out a folded piece of paper.

She drew a picture.

ART: That looks like you, wuss.

GUFF: Hey, it is me! Hold on.

He uncrumples a second piece of paper from his jacket pocket.

Here it is!

ART: That's him, is it? He's got three hands.

GUFF: No, that's a mistake, that is.

ART: Are those glasses?

GUFF: I don't know. Could be bags under the eyes, I suppose.

ART: How old is he?

GUFF: Forty three.

> *Pause.*

> An' he's going grey.

> *Pause.*

> Oh aye, and she hasn't seen him for a while so he may have lost the facial hair.

> *ART looks closer at the drawing.*

ART: So we're looking for a middle-aged, possibly beardless, pot-bellied, non-descript sort of a man who may or may not wear glasses.

GUFF: An' he's a good bit taller than me.

ART: Of average height.

GUFF: And he's white.

> *They both survey the pub.*

ART: *For fuck's sakes, they could all be him, mun!*

> *GUFF takes the drawing.*

GUFF: Hey, it looks a bit like a fat Noel Edmonds, doesn't it? No mun, I know, that bloke from Chas and Dave! Chas, is it, or/

ART: /Put it away, mun.

GUFF: Hang on, I'll find out if he's 'ere for you now.

ART: How?

GUFF: What's his name again?

ART: Gregory Towns/

GUFF: (*Shouting.*) *Greg oh!!*

    Everyone looks round. GUFF realises his mistake.

    Oh aye.

    Pause.

    Hey, got any cash on you, wuss? That was my last fiver.

ART: One day, Guff, I will so hurt you for what you just did.

GUFF: (*To BARMAN.*) Do you change cheques here, mate?

ART: Hopelesser and hopelesser.

GUFF: Tidy way to spend the day anyhows. Stop looking in the mirror, mun.

ART: I'm not.

GUFF: Look, don't despair wuss. For all we know, someone might walk through that door any second who looks more like this drawing than anyone else here. And then we'll know it's him, won't we?

    Pause.

    Hey up!!

ART: Where?

    GUFF points at two women who have just come in.

GUFF: There innit.

ART: Drag artist is he? You might have mentioned that, Guff.

GUFF: Look, as we're here, we may as well try and pass the time pleasantly. Test the old pulling power, innit. They look nice, mun, not too attractive, see. Less beauty, more hope – that's my motto.

ART: He's not coming, is he?

GUFF: Fuck him, mun.

Pause. Something occurs to ART…

ART: Unless he's here.

Scene 4

3.00 p.m. GUFF is alone at the bar with two more pints, finishing a bag of crisps and fiddling with a poem on a beer mat. Two of the previous customers are leaving. GUFF puts away the beer mat as ART comes towards the bar with an empty pint glass.

GUFF: Any joy?

ART: The one thing all the customers in here have in common is that none of them answers to the name of Gregory Arsehole Townsend.

GUFF: I asked the barman if he knew him.

ART: And…

GUFF: Yeh, he does. Only he said he doesn't come in here so much now. Not since he's got back with his wife.

ART: So the barman knows him?

GUFF: Yes.

ART: So he knows he's not in.

GUFF: Yes.

ART: And so do you.

GUFF: Yes.

ART: Well, thanks for not sharing that with me sooner, wuss. I'd hate to have missed out on making a complete prat of myself in front of total strangers, aye.

GUFF: Aye well, relax now innit? Lunch-time's long gone.

ART: Where's the Ugly Sisters then?

GUFF: Toilet. No, gone.

Pause.

Well, you buggered off and left me on my own with them.

ART: I got held up. I got talkin' to some bloke who thought I was Irish.

GUFF: Why?

ART: I don't know but if he comes over, I'm Seamus O'Shea from Donegal, right, and you're Guff from Wales.

Pause.

He liked my script, anyway.

GUFF: What does he do then?

ART: Fuck knows. Something to do with little bits of plastic. I couldn't understand him, mun. He was off his face. Kept spittin' on me when he spoke.

They drink.

GUFF: Cheers, wuss.

ART: I can't believe you wrote that woman a poem, wuss.

GUFF: Worked once, see.

ART: Did you make it up there and then?

GUFF: No, I made it up before.

ART: Cheat.

Pause.

Did he cash you a cheque, then?

GUFF: Aye. For a charge, like.

ART/GUFF: (*Together.*) Make a day of it, is it?

ART: Fuck Gregory Towsface, innit?

GUFF: Fuck him. And all his fuckin' lookalikes an' all.

ART: What the fuck did *Carlton* ever do anyway?

Scene 5

Pub. 9.30 p.m. ART and GUFF still propping up the bar, several pints on. A whole new clientele has come in. A group of young businessmen sit at the table by the toilets. GUFF is eating a packet of peanuts.

GUFF: See, those poets in the trenches – they've been there, 'aven't they, down the pit like, seen their best friends' face explode an' all that, lived day in day out with the stench of death, the unbearableness of life. So they had things to say, didn't they – horrors to speak of, terrible secrets to divulge. They had to write about it to make sense of it, didn't they? Because it was a damn sight better than holdin' it all (*Points to his head.*) in 'ere, see…

Pause.

Hey, don't look so bored by everything I say, wuss.

ART: Say something interesting, then.

GUFF: Listen then!

ART turns towards him, focuses on him.

Aye well, all I'm sayin' is that…don't stare at me like that, mun.

ART folds his arms and stares at the bar.

ART: This listening stance alright for you?

GUFF: Lost my track now, anyway.

ART: Trenches…poets…explodin' faces…

GUFF: Oh aye, no, what I was sayin' was that.. sometimes
I wish I could have a nervous breakdown, see.

ART: I think I'm having one now, wuss.

GUFF: I haven't been down the pit, see, looked the serpent
in the eye. Remember Mathew Pryce, just after his O
levels? Hospitalised, mun, broken, never to recover
really, properly. All they did was patch him up mentally,
stuck him back together like a broken cup, mun, cracks
all on show. He used to sit in the corner of the Prince's
Head, remember, all white-faced and old before his time,
and he hardly spoke. Only when he did see, everyone
listened. Cos they all wanted to know what he had to say
after his little trip to Hell.

Pause.

Only he said there were no serpents, see, it wasn't even
dark. Too light if anything – sort of everyday. Only more
everyday than anything else – everything the same apart
from him. Unable to bear any of it and not knowing why.

Pause.

But I don't know, see. I don't find day to day life that
horrific. I'm too benign in my bastard soul, see. I'm a
contented man at the end of the day, not deep enough,
see, that's my problem. Trouble is…nothing's wrong.

ART: Or everything is.

GUFF: Hey, sorry, mun.

ART: What for?

GUFF: I didn't mean to, I mean, that must have sounded terrible.

ART: Forget it.

GUFF: See, I don't think of what happened to you as a breakdown as such – more a glitch, a temporary set-back. I mean, you never made it to hospital, did you?

ART: No, wuss. Much as I begged them to, the bastards just wouldn't let me in.

GUFF: Good. Cos you know I wouldn't have said all that/

ART: /Fuckin' hell, Guff, forget it mun. Stop making issues out of nothing, alright? Jesus.

ART lights a cigarette, smokes. GUFF watches him.

GUFF: Hey, do your dog eatin' a wine gum, wuss.

Slight pause before ART lapses into a curious impression of a dog chewing, stopping and contorting its face in order to prise the gum out of its teeth. GUFF guffaws somewhat over-excitedly. ART eyes him warily.

ART: Still find that funny, do you, wuss?

GUFF: Funny as fuck.

ART: Cos you wouldn't laugh if you wasn't funny, would you?

GUFF: No, mun. Duw, Duw.

ART: No point to that, see.

ART resumes the impression. GUFF's laughter is now somewhat panicked in its hysteria. ART joins in, finally convinced GUFF's amused.

Good as gold, dull as fuck, mun.

Pause.

This is what it's about see. I want to grow old, see wuss. I wanna be an old man at the bar tellin' stories, 'aving the crack in my cap and scarf with odd socks and slippers on. Cos they're comfy, not cos I'm goin' dw-lali-tap, like.

Pause.

Hmm…*dw-lali-tap*, mun!!

GUFF: I'd hate that. Shoot me first.

ART: I don't want to listen to no ticking clocks above diamond patterned carpets telling me it's time to take a queen cake from the tin and warm the bastard pot. If I can't go to the pub for a drink when I'm seventy nine, what's the bastard point of gettin' there?

GUFF: I'm comfortable in any pub, see, from your snottiest wine bars to your Workin' Man's Club, wuss. I've drank in some of the roughest dives, aye, but I've never been in a fight in my life. Seen some, mind. I know how to blend in, see. That's important for a writer, I think. Keepin' your head down, mixin' in all circles. Honest to God, there isn't a pub I wouldn't be happy to drink in, wuss.

ART: How about Gay bars, wuss?

GUFF: Pubs, mun, not bars.

ART: Gay pubs, then.

GUFF: Aye, I'd drink in one, like, no problem.

Pause.

Only thing with Gay bars though is, when you walk into one, the clientele automatically assume you're 'one of them' like.

ART: But you're Everyman, Guff. You just said. You blend in anywhere.

GUFF: Yeh but I wouldn't want to mislead anyone, would I? I meant pubs where people just go for a drink, like, not to cop off.

ART: So, what's your point then, wuss?

GUFF: I don't know any more.

Pause.

I'm not homophobic, mind.

ART: I know that, mun. You just don't want some bloke sticking his tongue down your throat cos you gave off signals you didn't know existed.

GUFF: Yes.

ART: That aside, you're perfectly content to mix with all sorts, regardless of class, race or culture.

GUFF: Yes.

Pause.

Apart from racists.

Pause.

And Germans.

ART: And thieves.

GUFF: I hate thieves.

Pause.

It was a crap point to make, thinkin' about it.

ART: No, you were doin' fine till I butted in. Sorry, wuss, I feel bad now. I didn't mean to pick holes in what you were sayin'.

GUFF: No, mun, that's what chat is.

ART: Aye, be hell of a world if we all sat and nodded in mutual consent.

GUFF sits and nods.

Some people are uncomfortable in silence, see.

Silence.

I'll be back now.

ART leaves, passing a crowd near the toilets.

Alright, gents?

ART is about to enter the toilet when they erupt into laughter. He stiffens for a second, then walks on.

GUFF reaches into his pocket and gets out his biro and a beer mat on which is written a poem. He starts reworking it.

GUFF: (*Reading.*) Your eyes belie a wanton lust...
Your eyes belie a wanton lust... (*He chews his pen, thinks.*)
Lust... dust... trust... (*He writes, pleased.*)
... broke my tender teenage...(*Barely audible.*)... trust.

ART returns, watches GUFF for a short while before he approaches.

Your flies are undone.

ART: You've got a face like a smacked arse but at least I can do my flies up.

GUFF: No need for that. Don't get so defensive, mun.

ART: No. I shouldn't, should I? What have I got to be defensive about? I'm nearly forty years old and I'm standing in a bar kiddin' myself that I'm some sort of talent when all I really am is a spineless failure with bad guts and a ten a penny screenplay that no fucker wants to read, let alone make. Gregory fuckin' Townsend – he didn't even let me down, wuss. He doesn't even know I exist. Do the words 'goose' and 'chase' spring to mind?

And 'straws' and 'clutch'? It's a joke, see. Only no-one's laughin'. Cos it's not that fucking funny!

GUFF: Hey, c'mon now, wuss.

ART: See, I don't even know if I mean what I say. In fact, I probably don't. Cancel it. Forget it. I'm goin' to go over there and arrive here all over again, only this time I won't whine on like the self-piteous arsehole I've become. Alright?

ART walks a few paces, before approaching the bar.

Alright, Guff, this for me is it?

ART picks up the pint, drinks a little and then pours it over his head.

Hell of a boy see, me! Still find that funny, do you, wuss?

GUFF: C'mon wuss, let's go home.

Blackout.

Scene 6

The flat, later the same night. GUFF enters eating the remains of a bag of chips. He pointedly holds the door open for ART. ART walks through reading a letter.

ART: 'The style is inventive and the writing both lively and intelligent. However the narrative rambles somewhat and there is no distinctive sense of jeopardy for the protagonist. Blah, blah, regret to say that we have no suitable slots for this piece as it stands. Yours, Gregory – I didn't come to the pub today because I was too busy dictating this rejection letter – Townsend'.

GUFF: Never mind, mun.

ART crumples up the letter and looks at GUFF reworking his poem on the beer mat.

ART: If the relentless rejection of my screenplay does
    nothing but inspire you to write, my friend, then I am
    fulfilled. 'Narrative jeopardy', my arse. Done one poxy
    'How to write a screenplay' course and thinks he knows
    the bastard lot. I'm amazed he didn't mention the classic
    'three act construction'.

Pause.

Or lack of it.

GUFF: (*Re poem.*) Hey, this is alright, this.

ART lights a cigarette.

Pause.

ART: Read it to me.

GUFF: Is it?

ART: Can I bear it? What's it about?

GUFF: I wrote it first for Maisie Banks.

Silence.

Remember her? My first love. All goin' swimmingly till
    you copped off with her at my mother's wake.

ART: Sorry, wuss. If it's any consolation, she cried after.
    Guilty black tears.

GUFF: Ah well, no matter, it's history, mun. I got used to
    it. They all fancied you, really. I like this laundry
    woman, Kaye. She's a fighter, see. I like that.

ART: I'll lose you to the soap suds, mate, and die here rejected.

GUFF: Don't be soft, mun. I just like her is all.

GUFF holds up the beer mat.

Right…hey, I feel a bit self-conscious now, wuss.

ART: Thing is with Maisie Banks, she used to fart, remember, and sniff the air and go, 'Mmm, chocolate', or 'Mmm, strawberry'. I couldn't be doin' with that, mun.

GUFF: Or 'raspberry' innit? Aye, Maisie could fart for Wales. Right/

ART: /It put me off, mun. I never saw the humour in it. I hate all that communal farting camaraderie.

GUFF: I assumed that. That's why I try to restrain mine. Out of respect, like.

Pause.

Funny thing is, there's me on the couch trying not to fart when you're wanking away under the sheets to your heart's content.

ART: Fuck off.

GUFF: But you do, mun.

ART: Guff, I'm waiting to be both humbled and devastated by your poetic genius over 'ere.

GUFF: I can hear you, though.

ART: Bollocks.

GUFF: I can, mun.

ART: Guff, how come you can hear me when you always fall asleep before me?

GUFF: I don't.

ART: You do.

GUFF: Well, maybe I wake up again/

ART: /D'you know how I know you're asleep? Cos you start laughin', that's how, wuss, I'm tellin' you. Night after night I listen to you lyin' there laughing with your arms crossed over your chest, like this.

ART does a pretty accurate impression.

GUFF: No! In my sleep?

ART: Aye. It drives me bananas, mun. Smug chuckles nearly every bastard night. So you really don't know you're doin' it then?

GUFF: No, wuss, honest to God.

Pause.

Hey, what do I do? Do me again?

ART repeats impression.

Happy like that, is it? Duw, Duw. I wonder what I'm laughin' about.

ART: I wish I knew, wuss. At least then I could share in the bastard joke. Keeps me awake, see.

GUFF: Oh, that's why you wank, is it? Somethin' to do? I mean, at least I don't know I'm laughin' see, innit?

ART: Look, I don't wank!

GUFF: Aye, aye, if you say so. Just wait till I'm out or do it in the bathroom, innit/

ART: /*I DON'T WANK ALRIGHT!*

GUFF: I don't mind, mun.

ART: How can you mind something *I DON'T FUCKING DO!*

GUFF: Alright, mun. Hmm, the words 'lady' and 'protest' spring to mind.

ART: You want to watch that.

GUFF: (*Re poem.*) You ready to hear this, then?

ART: What? Oh, that. I don't know. I was ready before.

GUFF: Good, cos the shock of you finally listening to one of my poems might well have killed me.

ART: Tomorrow, wuss.

GUFF: Aye, aye.

ART: Look, read it now, then.

GUFF: Not under duress. Not if you're not in the mood, no.

GUFF undresses, turns out the light. ART lies on his bed.

ART: Sorry.

GUFF: No matter.

ART: Sorry about earlier an' all. In the pub, like. Had a bit of a wobbler there.

GUFF: It's alright. Waste of good beer, 'at's all.

ART: That used to be your party trick.

GUFF: Aye, when I was a fifteen-year-old tosspot.

ART: Point taken.

GUFF settles on the couch. He chuckles.

What?

GUFF: I don't know. The idea of me chucklin', mun.

ART: I have created a monster.

GUFF: We 'ave a laugh though, wuss.

ART: You do.

GUFF: Aye mun, big pair of schoolkids, the pair of us.

Pause.

Hey! You know your screenplay. You're not worried that no-one will like it, are you?

ART: Well, no.

Pause.

At least I wasn't till you said that. Till you planted seeds of doubt in my head.

GUFF: Oh, sorry wuss. Hmm…seeds of doubt. What do they grow into, then?

ART: Doubtflowers. Trees of mistrust. Shrubs of suspicion.

GUFF: Doubtflowers. I like that.

ART: Aye, and they look like this.

ART rises up, tilts his head and pulls a face.

Lips pursed, eyes askance, heads tilted.

GUFF: Don't water them then, wuss.

ART: Don't plant them, then.

Pause.

Petals of paranoia.

GUFF: Hmmm.

GUFF settles, quietly snoozes.

After a bit, ART rises, lights a cigarette with a new lighter, and goes to sit on the stool by the window.

ART: I felt good at the bar with you today, wuss, golden lager, silver tongue. That lovely liquid plateau of 'drunk'. Swung into the gents, see, greeted some lads as I passed.

Pause.

Then I heard it, then it hit…a laugh…someone's laugh, not just any old laugh but the kind of laugh that knocks cold into the base of your spine.

And I thought, 'Nah, just being silly, don't even know 'em' and then the little demons in my head said, 'But Art, just because you're paranoid doesn't mean that everyone doesn't really hate you'... And there was a rush of silence in my ears , limbs like lead suddenly as all the guile and the stroll fell away...and I was in the mirror, looking, searching...eyes all pale and pink and puffy – fat pet rabbit eyes, staring at...nothing. No-one home. Hollow. Then the lips moved and they told me to hold on. 'Hold on', they said.

Pause.

To what, though?

Long pause. He smokes.

Night mun. Freaks me out. Moments that stretch like months.

ART finishes his cigarette, remains on the stool in the semi-darkness. Time passes. GUFF stirs on the couch.

GUFF: Will you come to the funeral?

ART: I can't, wuss.

Pause.

I can't face them.

GUFF: This isn't about you, Art. It's about Auntie Jo and what she meant to me. Whether you've made it or not won't even cross people's minds.

ART: No, cos I won't be there.

GUFF: Your Mam'll be sorry.

ART: Tell her I've got a meeting I can't miss, alright?

Pause.

Guff?

GUFF: My Dad said he's got a couple of suits we can borrow.

ART: Your Dad's five foot three, Guff. I'm not goin' to no funeral lookin' like Norman Bloody Wisdom.

GUFF: Art/

ART: /Guff! Subject closed! Capice?

Pause.

Do some writing tomorrow.

GUFF: Might nip to the launderette.

ART: Hey, you must have the best-washed pants in Britain, wuss.

No response. ART looks up, out of the window.

No stars.

GUFF: Nos da.

ART: (*Smiling.*) Night then.

GUFF settles back. ART lights another cigarette. Silence.

GUFF: I wish you'd come, Friday.

ART: Aye, alright. We'll see, is it?

Scene 7

The Flat. Friday. Midday.

GUFF's hold-all is gone. ART sits on the bed in his underwear, rubbing his head. Silence.

The flat door starts rattling. ART looks up.

It rattles some more, then, starts to open. ART runs to the bathroom. The flat door breaks open. NICKY stands there with ART and GUFF's kitchen knife. SUES follows him in. They are a little giggly and spaced-out.

SUES: Nice to make use of the studio space occasionally, darling.

SUES wanders into the kitchen as NICKY goes to the hi-fi and checks out the small CD pile. NICKY selects 'Portishead' and plays it quietly.

SUES picks up a packet of peanuts, starts eating them as she opens the fridge door.

NICKY lights a half-smoked joint from his cigarette tin with ART's lighter and sits in the wicker chair.

SUES: Want some juice?

NICKY: (*In cod Welsh accent.*) No, but I'd love a cup of tea, our Mam.

SUES laughs as she switches on the kettle.

SUES: And when are Bill and Ben due back?

NICKY: Tonight, tomorrow probably. After they've laid dear old Auntie to rest, they'll no doubt feel obliged to weep into their beers a little and pay their respects with a good old rousing sing-song. (*Re joint.*) Want any of this?

SUES takes it, smokes.

SUES: I had the strangest dream last night. I dreamt I saw my mother.

NICKY: Underwater or on dry land?

SUES: Both. She looked very young.

NICKY: Perhaps her hold on you is regressing as you mature. It's a good sign, Sues.

SUES: You were in it.

NICKY: What was I doing?

SUES: Oh, just sitting in a chair talking crap. No surprises there.

NICKY: I may have appeared ineffectual to you at the time, Sues, but I was probably a tremendous source of comfort. That's probably why you bade me into your dream.

SUES: 'Bidden or Unbidden, God is There'.

She hands NICKY the joint. He takes it, reaches for her hand.

NICKY: For you, always.

She moves away. He watches as she picks up one of ART's books, flicks through it.

SUES: Ah, look, he's circled something, 'The creative process taking place in bad artists may be much the same as the creative process in good artists, although its results may not be valuable for anyone other than the bad artist himself'. D'you think our Art has a good artist/bad artist complex?

NICKY: I wouldn't be surprised. Strikes me as a man of many neuroses – all of them dull and provincial. A little knowledge is a dangerous thing. Dylan Thomas has a lot to answer for.

Who was it that said, 'Show a Welshman a hundred doors and he will go through the one marked 'Self-destruct'?' Burton, I think.

Pause.

'Nothing is so poor and melancholy as art that is interested in itself and not its subject'.

SUES: Do you just make those up?

NICKY: I wish.

SUES holds up another book.

SUES: 'How To Make A Successful British Movie'.

NICKY: Don't take that. Him not having it could have a devastating effect on the future of the British Film Industry.

SUES laughs as she sets it on the hi-fi. She goes through the drawers.

SUES: Hey, socks with funny wee messages on them! 'What is one…without the other?' Ah, that's sweet.

NICKY: I'll give Mariette a bell later. She said she might drop round Sunday. She's got some wicked grass, apparently.

SUES: Good. Will she get us some 'e' as well?

NICKY: We still owe her for last time.

SUES: Ah well, you could always pay her in kind. Just be careful you don't catch anything, right?

NICKY: (*Softly.*) Hey come here.

SUES: Why should I come to you?

NICKY crosses to the sofa, sits by her. They kiss. She pulls away.

Oh, but not now. Later, eh? Tonight. (*She gets up.*)

NICKY: Oh yeh, you wouldn't want to be too sober, darling. You might feel something.

SUES: (*Sharp.*) Before you start getting at me, consider this. Did you screw her cos I wasn't putting out, or did I stop putting out when you started fucking her?

Pause.

Jees, I come all this way from home, I break all those ties and I still stand here sounding like my bloody mother.

She stands, disappointed by her own anger. NICKY sighs.

NICKY: Sues, it meant nothing.

SUES: Sorry, I keep forgetting we have this bond that transcends betrayal.

She stops herself again. NICKY rubs his eyes. SUES hovers – how to rescue this now? He won't look at her. He smokes the last few puffs of his joint, stubs it out.

SUES whips on one of GUFF's stripey tee-shirts, sticks a cushion up it and puts a bobble hat on her head. She comes up behind NICKY and hurls herself on top of him over the sofa.

(*In a mock Welsh accent.*) Want a fuck, is it darling? Well, get your knickers off, love. I 'aven't got all day.

She lunges dramatically and emits a loud roar.

Oops, too late. All done.

They roll onto the floor, kiss a little.

NICKY: So when ever did you fuck a Welshman, then?

SUES: (*Pulling out the cushion.*) Oh, the other night. Well, not a fuck per se. I read Art's script out to him and he had a bloody good wank.

They kiss more intimately.

Will you give her up?

NICKY: No sooner said, babes.

SUES: Let's go downstairs, eh?

She picks up a half full bottle of whiskey.

Shall we take this?

NICKY: Nah, that's cheap shit.

Pause.

I am sorry, you know, about Mariette.

SUES: Good. Wear this for me tonight…

She throws him ART's crumpled silk shirt.

…and we can pretend it's 1989 and we've only just met.

She takes the book, the kitchen knife and the shirt. NICKY turns and carefully picks his joint stub out of the saucer before unplugging the hi-fi and following her out.

A few moments pass.

Very slowly the bathroom door opens inch by inch. ART looks round. There is a sudden noise downstairs.

ART: Shit!

He disappears back into the bathroom.

End of Act One.

ACT TWO

Scene 1

The Flat. Two days later. Late afternoon.

The flat is seemingly empty. The curtains are shut. The whiskey bottle is now empty and a bottle of sherry stands next to it on ART's crate. The locks on the door are fixed and there is a new Chubb lock fitted onto the door. Footsteps are heard climbing the stairs. They pause outside the door. There is a bang on the door, then the unmistakeable voice of a very jovial hungover GUFF is heard outside.

GUFF: (*Off.*) Allwrong!! Let us in, Artie baby, if you're there. My hands are full.

> *There is sudden movement from beneath a pile of clothes and blankets on ART's camp-bed. ART looks at the door.*

ART: Guff?

GUFF: C'mon, I'm wasted, wuss.

> *ART emerges in jeans and sweat-shirt. He unlocks the chubb lock and opens the door. GUFF enters in a black suit, wearing sunglasses. He carries his holdall and two carriers and three letters. He dumps everything on the sofa. He takes off his shades.*

Bit dark in 'ere, innit? Christ, you look like I feel, wuss. Nothin's real.

> *GUFF puts his sunglasses back on.*

Hey, d'you reckon I look like Harvey Keitel in these?

ART: Where've you been, Guff? It's Sunday.

GUFF: Aye, sorry about that. They wouldn't let me go, mun. Crackin' funeral though. Ate too many cakes, mind.

ART: Guff…

Pause.

Did you read out your poem, then?

GUFF: No, not in front of that bunch of plebs. Pearls before swine, mun. Hey, you should see what I've got 'ere, wuss. Supplies!! Food and drink.

GUFF pulls out a bottle of whiskey and tequila, both nearly full from a carrier bag.

Should keep us goin' for a bit, see. Actually, the spirits aren't so much supplied as nicked from the back of my Auntie Ray's Christmas cupboard. I'll pay her back though, see. Good innit?

ART: Great, mun.

GUFF: Got your mail 'ere an' all.

ART: Thanks. Must have missed these.

GUFF chucks the letters at ART, one of which is large and padded, goes to the kitchen and pours a glass of water and gulps it down.

GUFF: Oh, needed that. Did my giro come then, Friday?

ART: No.

GUFF: Shit. Ring 'em tomorrow. Kick some arse.

Pause.

What you been up to, then?

ART: Growing my hair.

GUFF: Hey, they were all askin' after you. Your Mam wants to know how your meetin' went. Made me phone, mun. Couldn't get an answer, though. Out roisterin', were you? Anyway, the woollies are in the bag. Completion of

the second batch is imminent. Did you miss me laughin'
then, wuss? Or were you too busy spankin' the old
monkey in peace, like?

Pause.

You goin' to open those or what?

*ART looks at envelopes, slowly opens one. GUFF rises, opens
the curtains.*

Let some light in, is it? Aye, the boys reckoned I was the
spit of Harvey Keitel, see. Kept callin' me 'Harve', mun.
I quite liked it actually. Better than 'Guff', innit?

Pause.

What's those then, wuss?

ART: Two more 'No's and one's had the kindness to return
my script. Great, I can draw pictures on the back.

GUFF: Send it out again, mun.

ART: Is there anyone left?

GUFF: Course, mun and we'll be meetin' some of 'em
sooner than you think, wuss. Ask me why?

ART: If I do, do you promise not to answer.

Pause.

Guff, that demented smile on your face is seriously quite
disturbing.

GUFF: Ask me why, then.

ART: Why is your face contorted thus?

GUFF: Because I've got some *good news!*

*ART holds a cushion over his head. GUFF ploughs on,
regardless.*

I popped into the launderette just now, see, just to tell Kaye how it all went, like. Anyway, turns out there's this party on tonight that she can get us into and there should be…

GUFF goes over to ART and removes the cushion, banging it over art's head for emphasis.

…*loads of contacts there for us.* And, she also told me that she absolutely loved my poems so much she's already set one to music *and* she's plannin' on singing it tonight at said party. Not bad, eh?

ART: Good, mun. Good for you.

GUFF: Hey, she gave me a rough copy of the song, like. Have a listen, shall we?

GUFF reaches into his jacket pocket and produces a cassette.

Where's the…? Where's the hi-fi, wuss?

ART: It's… I took it to be repaired.

GUFF: No! What was wrong with it, then? I only just bought it a month ago, mun. What did they say?

ART: Dust trapped in the…

GUFF: In the what?

ART: Oh look, I'm sorry, Guff.

GUFF: Not your fault.

ART: No, it's…not that. It's… I don't want to lie to you. It's not being repaired. It's…don't go ape on me now, right, but we got burgled. It's been stolen.

GUFF: No.

Pause.

When?

ART: Friday, wuss.

GUFF: Where were you?

ART: Down the Crown, wuss, drinking to Auntie Jo's memory. When I got back, the bastard door was hangin' open. They forced the lock, see. I got it fixed up yesterday, though, got a new Chubb lock put on. There, see.

ART rises and points it out. He takes a spare key from the top drawer.

Here you are. Should be safe now.

GUFF: Bit bloody late now though, innit.

Suddenly GUFF kicks the sofa hard.

Shit! I hate theft!!

Pause.

What did the police say?

ART: Not much hope.

GUFF: Did anyone else get done?

ART: Haven't seen anyone.

GUFF: No insurance either.

GUFF hits himself across the face.

Twat! You fucking twat, Guff!!

ART: I'm sorry, wuss.

GUFF: What d'you keep apologising for?

ART: Well, cos you're upset. Look, I know how you feel about theft, wuss.

Pause.

What?

GUFF: Just wondering.

ART: Wondering what?

GUFF: Just wondering why you're looking so bastard guilty
is all. I'm not bein' funny now, wuss, but you are runnin'
a bit low on funds just now. You 'aven't gone and bastard
sold it, have you, and then concocted this whole burglary
story/

ART: /Fuck off mun, Guff/

GUFF: /Cos you didn't exactly come straight out with it and
it does look as though it's the only thing that's been had.

ART: And my silk shirt.

GUFF: (*Screaming.*) Did your poxy silk shirt cost you two
hundred and sixty-nine pounds, did it? Did it?

ART: No.

> *Pause.*

> Hey c'mon wuss, I can't believe you think I'd pull a
> stunt like that. That's hurtful that is.

GUFF: Aye, I suppose. Sorry, wuss.

> *Pause.*

> Shit, shit and fucking shit!!

ART: They only took the one CD.

GUFF: 'Prodigy'?

ART: 'Portishead'.

GUFF: I was really startin' to get into that. Bastards. I could
kill 'em, see wuss. Bare hands, honest to fucking Christ!!
I hate theft!

> *GUFF punches the chest of drawers hard where the hi-fi
> used to be.*

It should still be here, mun! It should be sittin' here playin' my bastard tape with my poem on!

He sits, hunched, deep in thought. Suddenly he leans back.

Oh well. That's that, then. Nothin' to be done now, is there?

ART: You alright?

GUFF: Aye, life goes on, innit?. Hey, Sue and Nick must have a tape deck. I could play it there.

ART: They've gone out.

GUFF: Oh, right.

Pause.

Right. You fit?

ART: For what?

GUFF: This party, innit. I'm in need of a top-up after this. Pint should do it. Two day wake, mun and this!

ART: That's you done being angry, is it?

GUFF: Bad for my blood pressure, mun.

ART: And incessant drinking isn't?

GUFF: More fun though, innit. You comin' then?

ART: I don't know, wuss. Feel a bit wiped-out to tell the truth.

GUFF: Oh, c'mon Art, don't worry about me, mun. We've got to go. It's a combined Wrap Do or something so there'll be directors, producers, everything. Worth a try, see, so best kegs on and out to impress, innit. Need a swill an' all, sweating like a pig in a sauna, mun. We're goin' to meet up with Kaye's crowd in The Crown, alright?

ART: Do you trust me to meet her then?

GUFF: Yeh, she's not your type.

GUFF looks at his watch, gets his washbag from his holdall.

Shit, we should have been there by now. There's some Bara Brith in the Tesco bag if you fancy.

ART: But I don't know them, Guff. I don't know how to talk to washerwomen.

GUFF: Duw, you're a snob, aye.

GUFF goes into the bathroom.

ART: I know. See, that's the problem. I'll end up pretending that I find laundry work really fascinating, to compensate for the fact that I think it's beneath me. It happens every time.

GUFF: (*Off.*) Talk about yourself, then. That's what you normally do.

ART: Hello, I'm Art and I write screenplays no-one wants to make.

GUFF: (*Off.*) Don't be so negative.

ART half-heartedly mouths this.

You make your own luck, wuss. What you've got is good. Fuck the people who haven't got the talent to see it themselves.

ART: Thanks for the pep talk, coach.

GUFF comes out, shirtless. He lifts a laundered pile of stripey tee-shirts out of his holdall. He puts one on.

GUFF: Your Mam did these for me.

ART: Look at you, so excited. You're like a dog about to go 'walkies' in the park. New kegs?

GUFF: My Dad's.

GUFF sits to change his socks.

Hold up!

GUFF produces the hi-fi remote control from the side of a sofa cushion.

Well by damn. Think our little light-fingered friends left a little something behind. Well, that's a third of its value gone for starters. Cos it's a fuckin' pain in the arse havin' to get up every time you want to change the fucker, believe you me. Well ya-boo-sucks with bells-on to bastard burglars everywhere.

He kisses the remote and shoves it back into the sofa.

That's cheered me up, that. Ready?

ART: I don't know if I'm up to goin' out, Guff.

GUFF: C'mon, Art. Don't do this to me now.

ART: What?

GUFF: Come, mun. Look, I'm sorry I shouted earlier, alright?

ART: It's not that.

GUFF: What then? What's wrong?

ART: Do you think I write like Dylan Thomas?

GUFF: No.

Pause.

Why? Do you want to?

ART: Christ, no.

GUFF: Well you don't. You've got your own style. Right, you comin' or not?

ART: Um…

GUFF: *For Christ's sake, mun!* Art, please, I'm going.

ART: No! Don't! Hang on a sec, right? Just freshen up.

ART dashes into the bathroom, GUFF checks his reflection, slips the new key into his pocket, stares briefly at where his hi-fi sat, recovers, sings briefly.

GUFF: (*Singing.*) 'Stranger in the night. You're strange in daytime but you're stranger in the night.'

Pause.

C'mon Art! Chop, chop!

Pause.

Art?

ART: (*Off.*) Listen mate, you go! I'll join you down there, okay?

GUFF: Art! Open up!

After a pause, the bathroom door opens.

ART: Look at me. I'm in dire need of repair.

GUFF: Art/

ART: /Go Guff.

Pause.

Please, go.

GUFF: Are you alright, though. I mean you've got me worried, now. I wasn't yellin' at you/

ART: /I know. I'll be fine.

GUFF: I might miss 'em, see.

ART: I know.

GUFF: Will you come?

ART: Yes, I'll see you there.

GUFF: Promise?

ART: Promise.

GUFF waits a while. Art nods to the door. GUFF goes. The door shuts. ART looks at himself in the mirror. He ducks a little to find the angle.

C'mon Art boy. Still lookin' good in a bloodshot… haggard…beaten kind of a way.

ART opens the bottle of whiskey discarded on the couch and swigs. He picks up his coat, throws it on, lights a fag, and goes to the door. He opens it. He stops. He shuts the door and locks it from the inside. He sits on the floor for a long time. The light dims.

There is a knock on the door. ART doesn't move. Another knock.

NICKY: (*Off.*) Art? Yeh, we just saw Guff go out so we gathered you were up here all on your tod.

ART reaches for the bottle. It topples, makes a noise.

Art? Any chance of being let in?

ART goes to the bathroom. He flushes the toilet, goes to the door.

ART: Coming.

ART unlocks the door. NICKY and SUES stand there. They are glassy-eyed, more animated than usual. ART turns on the light.

NICKY: May we come in?

ART: Yeh, though I'm going out in a bit, mind.

NICKY: No sweat.

NICKY holds out the kitchen knife.

Yours, I believe.

ART: (*Taking it.*) Yeh, ta.

NICKY: You okay?

ART: Yeh, yeh, bit all over the place, you know. We only just got back, see, from the funeral. Should have known it would turn into a weekender, really.

NICKY: But Guff said you didn't go.

ART: No, that's right, but he told me about it in such vivid detail, I keep thinking I did…go there. Spoke to him, did you?

NICKY: Yeh, shame about the burglary, mate.

ART: Yeh well, only a crappy hi-fi, innit?

SUES: Did you call the police?

ART: No. What's the point, innit? I told Guff I had, though. It was his hi-fi, see, and he hates theft, well, you know, losing stuff he's bought.

NICKY: Yeh, we got done as well. Telly, video, the usual. It was all rental gear, anyway. Kids, I expect.

Pause.

Well, at least, they left your scripts. I got all my paintings nicked once. That was the pits. Those were something you couldn't put a price to, you know what I mean?

NICKY goes into the kitchen and switches the kettle on.

SUES: So, when d'you think it happened, cos we've been away?

ART: Friday afternoon, well, or morning or night maybe. I don't know. I was out all day. Got in really late.

NICKY: Makes sense. We got back Saturday.

ART: Well, I'd better go and freshen up, I suppose.

ART rises clearing some of GUFF's clothes, subtly digging out the remote control. He leaves it by the tesco bag.

Guff's a messy bugger, aye.

ART picks up one of GUFF's stripey tee-shirts and heads for the bathroom.

NICKY: Mind if I rustle up a quick cuppa, mate. We're all out down below.

ART: No, help yourself. There's some cake in that Tesco bag an' all. Bara Brith, sort of currant loaf, if you fancy it.

NICKY: Cheers.

ART shuts the bathroom door. SUES waves the remote at NICKY before tucking it into her knickers. She finds the cake and takes it into the kitchen. She cuts a few pieces as NICKY kisses her neck and caresses her from behind.

Is that a remote in your panties or is there something I should know?

SUES: You're not funny.

NICKY: (*Calling out.*) D'you want some, mate?

ART: (*Off.*) No, ta. In a bit of a rush.

ART comes out in GUFF's tee-shirt and sees the remote is gone.

NICKY: You know, you're lucky you didn't catch them at it, mate. Burglars can get pretty nasty when cornered. Even petty thieves.

NICKY eats some cake as he stirs the tea. He has made two mugs.

Hey, this is good. You ever tried cocaine, Art?

ART: Yeh, once like.

SUES: Did you like it?

ART: No. Reckon my head's fucked up enough without messin' about with it.

NICKY: Maybe you tried the wrong stuff. Nothin' like good charlie for giving you a nice buzz.

NICKY hands ART a mug of tea.

Milk and sugar I presumed. Only you're lookin' a bit peaky, mate, which is why I asked.

ART: Oh, no thanks. Crooked as it may be, I'm quite partial to my nose.

NICKY: I love this guy. He cracks me up. Doesn't he crack you up, Sues?

SUES: It might help you write.

ART: So would a commission and I'd rather hold out for that, ta.

NICKY: Still waiting?

ART: Yeh, but I'm pretty hopeful, see. Had some positive responses to the script already.

SUES: Good.

NICKY: Hey, that was great cake.

ART: Have some more.

NICKY rises and gets another piece.

SUES: Where are you off to, then?

ART: This party. Some tacky media do. Should get off soon, really.

NICKY: Hey, sounds cool. Been a while since we partied, eh Sues?

SUES: Where's it at?

ART: Um, I'm not sure, I'm meeting Guff first.

NICKY: Where?

ART: The Crown.

NICKY: Yeh? We might pop along later.

ART: Yeh, won't be much though. I mean, I'm not sure if I'll go.

Pause.

To the party, like.

Pause.

Might just have a quiet pint. We'll see.

The doorbell rings.

NICKY: Mariette?

SUES: I'll go.

SUES leaves, leaving the door on the latch. NICKY gets a rollie out of a tin. ART goes to light it. NICKY takes the lighter from him, lights it. He pockets the lighter, strolls to the window.

NICKY: Am I keeping you?

ART: No, well, no, I've got five minutes.

ART gets out a cigarette.

Um?

NICKY lights it before pocketing the lighter.

NICKY: Bet you're missing your music, yeh? Bummer that. Sorry about this, mate, but the girl at the door, Mariette? Well, she's got a bit of a thing for me and Sues has got it into her head that there's something going down between us, you know, so it's best to keep out of the way. You got a girlfriend or boyfriend, Art?

ART: No. Um, no to a girlfriend, that is.

NICKY: Are you gay?

ART: No, that's what I mean. I'm straight...but without a girlfriend, at present.

NICKY: Just wondered.

Pause.

She can get a bit worked up, Sues, a bit over-imaginative. Must be the French blood in her. That's why we went away Thursday. I don't know, I take her to this lovely little place in Bath, wine and dine her, make long-lasting love to her and now she's even more convinced I'm playing away. Thinks I'm suffering pangs of guilt. Women, eh?

ART: Never understood 'em.

NICKY: Don't bother tryin' mate.

The phone rings downstairs.

Of course, there's times when I thank the Lord for that Gallic passion, you know what I mean, but all this provin' my love's beginning to take its toll on Big Jim and the twins, you get my drift?

NICKY holds his hands protectively over his penis.

I love her to bits but I could do with a break tonight. Don't mind if we tag along, do you?

ART: No, well, they're Guff's friends, mind. I haven't met them.

NICKY: You could do with the company, then, I expect.

NICKY flicks through a copy of ART's screenplay as SUES walks back in, smiles at NICKY.

SUES: Coast's clear, darling. Goodies received and paid for. Mariette's fine with the new arrangement. Less of a drag, she reckons. (*To ART.*) Oh, Art, she found this outside by the steps.

SUES hands him his 'How To Make A Successful British Movie' book.

It's yours, isn't it?

ART: Oh, that! Forgot I had that.

SUES: That was Guff on the phone, wanting to know if you were on your way.

NICKY: We could have a little smoke before we go, if you like.

ART: Um, I don't know.

NICKY: It's up to you.

ART: Thing is, I'm not sure if I'm going to go. I think I might stay here, do some writing.

NICKY: Oh, right, well no problem. If you do go, give us a knock, yeh?

SUES: And if you don't and you get lonely, you're welcome to come and visit us. You know, you do look tired, Art. You want to watch the boozin' darling. It breaks men overnight. See yous.

NICKY: Keep creatin' eh, mate!

They leave. ART checks properly that the remote has gone. He reaches for a cigarette. Another lighter taken. He locks the door. He turns out the light.

Scene 2

Flat. An hour has passed. It is dark. ART stands by the window, looking out. He is wearing GUFF's stripey tee-shirt, a cardigan and GUFF's joggers. He has drunk a fair amount of whiskey.

ART: A pitch for a short, dark film. Two boys come to London looking for the crack. One of them finds it.

He goes into the bathroom, leaving the door half open taking the whiskey with him. The flat door opens and GUFF enters. ART comes out to find GUFF standing there.

GUFF: You didn't come, then.

ART: Got nothin' to wear.

Pause.

Couldn't face it.

GUFF: Yeh, well, I might have known, I suppose. I mean, the one night I've got somethin' good to go to and you pull this on me. Art, for Christ's sake, mun.

GUFF turns on the light.

Hey, c'mon mun, Art. I hate to see you like this, all dead eyes. They're a good crowd. I was 'aving a great laugh.

ART: Why come back then?

ART passes GUFF and checks the door is shut.

See, you wake up four days on the trot and you think, 'God, I look rough'. On the fifth day, you realise, 'This is it. This is how I look now'. Just as the rain stops and starts in a certain place, it takes one week, five days even to grow old. And you know that all your future plans, however vague, will never come to pass. All those stored images – kids' wellies in the hallway, dinner parties round oak tables, fine wine, old friends who respect your talent, a companion touching your arm as she gently mocks you because she knows you yet still loves you…dying fires, rainy nights, awards gathering dust on cluttered shelves… That's all they'll ever be – shadow dreams. Cos you're thirty six already

and it didn't happen yet. And if not that, then what?
A bloody long wait in the cold.

ART lights a cigarette. He looks into the match-box.

Shit, thirteen left.

GUFF: When did you last sleep, Art?

ART: Days...days.

GUFF: Why? Bad dreams?

ART: Good dreams, Guff, good dreams. And then,
waking up.

GUFF: We're all lonely, Art. You should come out, meet
more lonely people...feel less alone. See, I've never been
able to get over men like you. You're talented, bright,
attractive – fuckin' lucky, let's be honest, but you always
feel that someone, your own selves probably, cheated
you of something.

Us ugly buggers, we get on with life, see. We know
where our fantasy ends and begins, anything's better
than what we were taught to expect. Not gettin'
stuck in some dead-end marriage, workin' my arse
off for pennies is an achievement for me. Not that
anyone's ever proposed to me, like...but, that's not
the point.

The point is that we're here, wuss – halfway there and
you've written a great script and it'll get done, see. And
the other thing is that thirty six isn't old, wuss. If you
died, people would say, 'And only thirty six, look, what a
tragic waste of a young life'. Innit? So shape up, wuss. A
screenplay's more than a few poxy poems so don't insult
me by seein' us as 'sad'.

ART: For a moment there, I thought you'd forgotten how to
stop talking.

GUFF: That's better, mun.

ART: Thanks, Doctor Guff.

GUFF: Now, keep smiling, see those dark thoughts for what they are and come to the bastard party with me. C'mon, I've got the address 'ere. Hey, I'll even let you keep my joggers on, wuss.

ART: Thing is, wuss, if we go, those fuckers downstairs want to come along.

GUFF: We won't tell 'em we're goin', then.

ART: They'll hear us pass, though.

GUFF: Well, we'll lose 'em once we're there.

ART: /Guff, don't go, please. Not yet, mun.

ART goes to the kitchen, gets two glasses and pours two whiskeys.

Stay and have a drink. It's early, see.

GUFF: It's gone ten.

ART: We'll go in a bit, then. Have a drink with me first.

ART hands GUFF a glass.

Dark thoughts, see, you're right, a few dark days is all, but I can't face going out there yet.

GUFF: This is important to me, Art. She'll be singin' my words.

ART: Yeh, but you know how these parties are, wuss. They don't get goin' till after midnight. We've got loads of time. Go later, is it?

Pause.

Hey, don't make me beg, mun.

GUFF: It's just/

ART: /Half an hour. Tops. Come on, down the hatch and we'll do some slammers, get us in a party mood.

ART downs his whiskey. GUFF sighs as he goes into the bathroom. ART immediately gets out the tequila and some salt.

Hey, know what I just remembered, wuss?

GUFF: (*Off.*) That we're all out of bog-roll? Great, started now see?

ART grabs an open box of tissues from under his bed, hands it in, gets another glass as GUFF's still has scotch in it.

ART: You and me when our parents let us go off for the weekend to that Eisteddfod, remember? Drinking vodka and milk cos we had nothing to mix it with… (*He lights some candles.*) And we convinced ourselves we might die if we drank it neat. Spent the whole time throwing up. (*He turns off the main light.*)

GUFF: (*Off.*) I haven't touched vodka since. No, come to think of it, I have.

ART pours out large tequilas, lights a cigarette, drinks.

ART: And we were scared of the dark.

GUFF: (*Off.*) Were we?

ART: Aye, so we spent the night swapping secrets to stay awake.

The toilet flushes. ART tops up his tequila, then GUFF's.

GUFF: *(Off.)* I made mine up.

ART: No!

GUFF comes out grinning.

GUFF: Couldn't have Motormouth knowing my innermost, could I? (*Sits and claps his hands.*) Come on 'en.

They lick the back of their hands, ART pours on salt, they down them. GUFF gags, sips some of his scotch to take away the taste, sits back.

GUFF: French skipping see, remember that?

ART: Big craze with the girls, mun. And that thing with their hands.

GUFF: Cat's cradle.

ART: Aye mun, little frayed pieces of string – kept finding 'em all over the house. There was a whole winter once when every time I went to put my shoes on, my bastard laces were missing.

GUFF: I 'ad a crush on your sister, see.

ART: I know, you ignored her for two years.

GUFF: Guinnie. (*Laughs.*) Haughty she was, see.

ART: Guinevere and Arthur, mun, I ask you.

GUFF: Golden times though, Art, sittin' in the Long Jump makin' plans.

ART: Is that your secret, wuss? My sister? Cos I knew that so it doesn't count.

GUFF: No mun. French skipping. I used to do it in my room, see. Used to put the elastic round two chairs, and prop one under the door handle so no-one could come in. I was good at it too, light on my feet, see. I loved it, mun.

Pause.

I was always better at doin' things when no-one was looking.

ART: That's why I'm so adept at masturbation, wuss.

Pause.

I never knew, mun.

GUFF: Well, it was a secret I couldn't risk getting out. Richard Jewell got beaten up once for doin' it with the Form Four girls in the yard, remember?

ART: I do, wuss. I gave the 'Scrap' call.

GUFF: His mistake, see, doin' it in public.

ART: He was pretty light on his feet an' all.

GUFF: Diamonds, mun. Thick white elastic bought new. The best, mun, dog's bollocks it was. Hours I was at it. I was so good, Art, so deft, and I couldn't tell a bastard soul.

ART: I wish you'd told me, wuss. You could have, you know.

ART pours out two large tequilas. They both lick some salt before downing their drinks. ART pours out two more.

GUFF: Aye well, history now.

Pause.

Why salt, then?

ART: God knows, wuss. Bladdered I am. Trashed.

GUFF: Fuck, aye.

ART: Six matches left, mun.

ART goes to light a cigarette as GUFF blows the match out.

GUFF: Five now.

ART: I can only hope that you're seriously embarrassed by what you just did.

GUFF: No, I only get embarrassed in front of people I respect.

GUFF rises, goes to the bathroom.

ART: Cheers, wuss.

GUFF: (*Off.*) Joke, mun. Well, we've missed the bastard party now, 'aven't we?

ART: There'll be others, wuss.

ART tops up GUFF's drink.

GUFF: (*Off.*) Aye, aye.

ART: Guff?

GUFF: (*Off.*) What?

ART: Read us a poem then.

GUFF comes out of the bathroom.

GUFF: No! Really?

ART: Aye, come on then.

GUFF: Which one?

ART: Any one.

GUFF gets his poem book from his jacket. He sits and squints at his own writing.

GUFF: Hey, wuss, I can't read, mun. I can't see the bastard words. they're crawling about like little spiders, mun.

Pause.

Shit. No good.

ART: See if I can.

ART grabs the book. GUFF snatches it back.

GUFF: No, mun. No.

ART: Hey, wuss!

GUFF: No, it's wrong. This is personal, wuss, like a diary, innit?

ART: But you show 'em to people.

GUFF: Some of 'em, not all of 'em.

ART: Pick out one for me to read, then.

GUFF: No, I don't trust you. You'll peep.

GUFF puts the book back in his jacket pocket.

ART: Well, can you remember one, then?

GUFF: I might fuck it up, though.

ART: Well, that's that then, innit. Shame, mun.

GUFF: All these years I've been wantin' you to ask, mun.

ART: Tomorrow, is it?

They lick salt, down drinks, ART refills glasses.

Silence, mun.

GUFF: Hey, those hippies liked my 'Ode to Maisie Banks', didn't they? Fair play to them.

ART snorts.

What was that for?

ART: What?

GUFF: That, that snort.

ART: I didn't snort.

GUFF: Yes you bloody well did, wuss. I said they liked my poem and you went... (*He repeats the snort.*)

ART: Didn't mean anything by it.

GUFF: Bollocks.

ART: God, one little noise/

GUFF: /Don't sit there givin' me that, wuss. That was pure scorn, that was. Why? Do you find it that ludicrous that someone could like something I wrote, or what?

ART: No mun. Honest, now. If I did snort, it was at them, alright?

GUFF: Why, cos they liked my poem?

ART: No, Guff. It's nothing to do with your bastard poem, alright? You mentioned the hippies. I don't like the hippies. I made a sound to that effect. It really doesn't hold up to any further analysis, wuss, believe me.

GUFF: Why don't you like 'em though?

ART: Cos they're arseholes is why.

GUFF: No, they're alright mun.

ART: Guff, you don't know the half of it.

GUFF: Half of what?

Pause.

C'mon, tell me.

ART: No, best not.

GUFF: Look wuss, you can't hint at stuff and then back-track on me. It's not fair. If you've got a secret, I want to hear it.

ART: Okay, okay. You should know, really.

Pause.

Oh, I don't know, Guff/

GUFF: /Listen Art, I missed a bastard party to stay in with you tonight so what should I fuckin' know?

ART: Alright, I'll tell you But you've got to promise me you won't shout and rant and rave.

Pause.

I mean it, Guff. Promise me.

GUFF: Cross my heart and hope to die. Alright?

ART: Those two downstairs?

GUFF: Nick and Sue, aye.

ART: They robbed us, wuss.

GUFF: Don't be so soft, mun. They weren't 'ere, and they got done and all. That's no secret, wuss, that's paranoia. And a fuckin' anti-climax an' all if you must know.

ART: Yeh? Only I knew it was them cos I was here, alright? I was in the bathroom when they broke in. I heard them.

Silence.

GUFF: You windin' me up?

ART: No.

GUFF: So, why didn't you come out, then?

ART: Because, well, there were two of them and... See, I knew it, that's why I didn't tell you sooner cos I knew you'd look at me like that!

GUFF goes to the flat door.

ART: Where you goin'?

GUFF: Fuckin' 'ave it out with them.

ART: No mun, wuss. You promised.

GUFF: Okay, I won't shout at them. I'll just beat the shit out of them.

ART: Don't, Guff.

GUFF: I'm not scared of them.

ART: No, but I am, alright? They're weird and they fuck with my head. They were up 'ere before tellin' me all sorts. He told me all about their sex life, mun.

GUFF: No!

ART: Straight up.

GUFF: What did he tell you, then?

ART: I don't know, it was all fuckin' bullshit games, wasn't it? All I'm sayin' is, just leave it, right? The hi-fi's long gone. You won't get it back. It's a lost cause cos you've got no proof, see.

GUFF: You were here, mun.

ART: You can't tell them that!

GUFF: Why not?

ART: You can't tell them I was hiding in the bathroom like a frightened kitten!

Pause.

GUFF: We could tell the cops, though.

ART: Are you serious? What, go to the Copshop three days after the event and tell our tale? And after the cops have finished laughin' in my face and callin' me a 'big girl's blouse', what will they do? I'll tell you what. They'll come round here, ask some questions and then bugger off – case closed, my word against theirs. Only now those two downstairs will know that it was me who grassed them up, and I'll end up six feet under in a fucking bin-bag, wuss. Either that or sinkin' to the bottom of the Thames in concrete shoes.

ART lights another cigarette.

GUFF: It's not your hi-fi though, is it?

ART: I'll get you one, alright? A better one. Tomorrow, I swear. I'll put it on my Access card. Now please Guff, sit down. Slam with me, mun.

ART pours out two large tequilas. Something occurs to GUFF.

GUFF: Since when 'ave you had an Access card, then?

ART: Ages. I save it for emergencies, like.

GUFF: I want a new CD an' all, mind.

ART: I'll get you a 'Portishead' CD as well, alright?

GUFF: I don't know. I found it a bit depressing to tell you the truth. We'll 'ave a look, see what's there, is it?

ART: Whatever. Hey, c'mon, drink.

GUFF drinks down his tequila.

GUFF: You should 'ave told me though, wuss. That cock and bull story about bein' out all day!

ART: You may not be aware of this, Guff, but you are ,to all intents and purposes, violently kleptophobic. Your hatred of theft borders on the psychotic. So, maybe you can understand why I didn't relish the idea of tellin' you that I was actually on the premises the whole time we were bein' robbed.

GUFF pours himself another drink and suddenly explodes.

GUFF: It's the *fucking injustice* of it, mun! Shittin' on your own doorstep, that's what it is. Arseholes! Cunts!

Pause.

Sorry, wuss, I hate usin' that word. I still think we should 'ave it out with 'em, see.

ART: Please, Guff.

GUFF: You're a scaredy-cat, aye Art.

ART: Cautious is what I am, Guff. No point lookin' for
trouble, is there? They don't like me, see. They said
stuff, said I was 'provincial' and 'neurotic'.

Pause.

And they called us 'Bill and Ben'.

GUFF: I'll give 'em Bill and bastard Ben.

*GUFF drinks, sits back. He emits a low noise, like a growl.
ART realises in time that GUFF is chuckling.*

In the bathroom, though!

ART: Fuck off! They were ages an' all. I was on the bog,
mun. I couldn't bastard move. The seat was imprinted on
my arse for eight hours after.

Both collapse into giggles.

And you never came back, then and I couldn't show
I was here, couldn't even flush the toilet, mun. I was
watchin' from the window, prayin' that they'd go out so
I could run downstairs and ring the bastard locksmith.
And then I had to wait for him, didn't I? Shittin' myself
the whole time thinking they might come back before
I could let him in.

GUFF: And to think I used to look up to you, aye!

ART: Don't say that, mun.

Pause.

Listen, wuss, did you ever tell them about me, you
know, doing the 'five knuckle shuffle' under the sheets,
like?

GUFF: Why the fuck would I tell them about your wanking
habit?

ART: Exactly.

Pause.

Hey, I thought at one point that they were having a 'quickie' in 'ere an' all.

GUFF: No! Why?

ART: Well, I heard him cry out, see, you know, like… (*He emits a pained ecstatic roar.*) Well it didn't sound as if he'd stubbed his bastard toe, at any rate.

GUFF: Fuck! *Ych a fi! No!* If he's come on my bedding, I'll whip him like a red-headed stepchild, honest to Christ!

GUFF bundles up the bedding and shoves it into a bin-liner in the kitchen.

They're druggies, mun, they could have all sorts. I've been sittin' on that, mun!

ART: You won't catch anything, mun.

GUFF: No, but it's the thought though, innit?

GUFF picks up his jacket off the sofa.

ART: Where you going?

GUFF: Nowhere.

ART: Fast.

GUFF lays his jacket on the floor.

GUFF: Well, we've got one comfort. We've still got the bastard remote control, mun.

Pause.

Is that why you wouldn't come out? Didn't want to run into them? Art?

ART: Lost the plot a bit, 'at's all.

Pause.

Glad you're back, Guff.

GUFF: I'm glad I know what was wrong.

Pause.

Listen wuss, there's something you should know. It's just…earlier, you know when you wouldn't come out, well I got a bit worried, like/

ART: /Look, wuss, I know, alright? But there's no need to worry, honest. I went down a bit, that's all. I don't know – been a rough few days between those wankers and all those rejections, got me feeling a bit of a worthless prick. But I can see the clearer picture now. I've remembered why I'm here. Forty's my deadline, see. If I don't make it by then, I'll give up, go home and never write a bastard line again. Not one…single…semi-colon…but it will happen for me, for us. There'll be other parties, wuss and I'll be out there networking with the best of 'em. I'll pitch from the rooftops if I have to, see.

Pause.

Hey, I've got a new idea an' all.

GUFF: Good, mun.

GUFF goes into the bathroom. ART fills up GUFF's glass.

ART: See, last time, I didn't have a script, see. Only dreams. No good, mun. An' I went under a bit cos of that.

The downstairs phone rings.

GUFF: (*Off.*) You took to your bed, mun, lay there like a corpse.

ART: Thought there was a monster under it till I looked and realised he was sitting in my bastard soul.

Pause.

Yeh well, that's past.

GUFF comes out, takes his drink.

GUFF: I was scared, wuss. I went out to do a poetry readin', remember, and you rang me in the bar and said you'd died and were in hell and they were right, there was no peace for the wicked.

The phone stops ringing.

ART: Fuckin' hell. Yeh, but it's not like that now, is it? We've had a good crack here so far. An' we're going to get there, Guff, both of us. And then we can go home with our heads held high, innit? Cos you believe in me, don't you?

GUFF: Course I do.

ART goes to GUFF, raises his glass.

ART: Yeah? To us, innit?

There is a knock on the door. Pause. GUFF answers. NICKY stands there.

GUFF: Alright?

NICKY: Yeh, girl called Kaye rang. She couldn't wait. Just wanted to tell you it got a good response and could you call her tomorrow. Here's the number.

NICKY hands GUFF a piece of paper.

GUFF: Yeah.

NICKY: Right.

NICKY turns to go.

GUFF: Oi, Nick, oh!

NICKY: Kee.

GUFF: Sorry?

NICKY: Nick-kee!

GUFF: Oh, right…um…

NICKY: What, mate?

GUFF: Um, nothing, no matter. Cheers, I mean, thanks for this.

GUFF holds up paper.

NICKY: No sweat. Any time. Enjoy the party.

NICKY leaves.

ART: Like the way you sorted him out, wuss.

GUFF: It'll keep, don't worry.

ART: Went well, then. That's great.

GUFF: Aye well, probably won't come to anything, but I got a phone number out of it. It's a start see, innit?

ART: Could be a good partnership.

GUFF: Aye, Tim Rice, me.

ART: I'm pleased, wuss.

GUFF: Hey, she sang my words, mun! I'm pretty chuffed about that.

GUFF downs his drink, pours another.

ART: Course she did and they loved them. And why not? They'll seek you out and make you a star, mun.

GUFF: Hey, don't go overboard, wuss.

ART: Well, just remember I believed in you, alright? I do though, Guff, straight up. And you believe in me, see. I hope so, anyway.

GUFF: You know I do, wuss. Contacts, see, that's all you need. Get yourself out there, talk to people.

ART: Aye, you're right. No use dwelling, is there? I might start looking for funding, see about putting it on myself, like.

GUFF: Good idea.

ART: Been thinking about it for a while. You could be in it.

Pause.

Hey, you don't laugh at me with Kaye, do you?

GUFF: Don't be soft, mun.

ART: I'm glad you stayed, wuss. Been a good night, good chat, and you've had good news an' all. Things are on the up!

ART lies down on his bed.

French skipping, eh? Our secret. Hey, my face is sliding off, mun.

Long Pause.

Too drunk to dream, see.

GUFF: I'm glad you're feeling more positive, Art.

Pause.

Listen, wuss, you know what I was sayin' earlier, about you bein' in a bit of a state and me bein' a bit worried. Well, seems silly now but I rang your Mam, gave her this address, and our number. I told her you'd probably be alright, that I'd look out for you, but she might ring tomorrow, just to put her mind at rest, like. Okay? Art? Hey, Art, c'mon, don't hate me now.

Pause.

Always stickin' my nose in, see. Sorry, wuss.

GUFF sees ART is asleep. He finishes his drink.

No bedding now…fuckin' beatniks.

Pause.

My giro, mun. They 'ad my…signature.

Pause.

Fuck!

GUFF gets up, staggers to the toilet, opens the door. He leans heavily against the doorway.

Oh, shit.

Blackout.

Scene 3

The Flat. Next morning. The phone downstairs rings. ART is lying in the same position as the night before. GUFF lies in the bathroom doorway. ART stirs, very, very rough. After some time he notices GUFF on the floor, face down.

ART: Never again. Hey, Guff oh, you're sleeping on the floor, mun.

The phone stops. ART rises, steps over GUFF and goes into the bathroom.

(*Off.*) Jesus, on the wagon, wuss, for ever.

ART comes out with a glass of water, pokes GUFF with his foot.

Guff oh! Guff oh, c'mon, come to.

Pause.

You've been sick, wuss. Guff! Guff?

ART rolls him over, puts water to his mouth, lifts his head.

C'mon, donkey boy, c'mon!

GUFF is still.

Oh no, no, no… C'mon, wuss. Wake up mun, you've got a date.

ART pours water onto GUFF's face – nothing. ART feels for his pulse, nothing. He starts to pump his heart. It is useless. GUFF is dead.

ART sits for a long time… Suddenly he starts packing everything into a holdall – his clothes, scripts, books, shoes, toiletries from the bathroom. He puts on his coat, heads for the door. He stops. What is he doing?

He catches himself looking in the mirror.

He goes to the sofa. GUFF's holdall is still on it. He reaches in and pulls out a brown paper parcel. He opens it – three bright, woolly jumpers.

Guff oh, wake up, you've got a date.

Pause.

What happened, wuss?

ART reaches for GUFF's jacket still on the floor. He takes GUFF's poem book out of the pocket. He pulls out his fags. One last match. He lights it and opens the book.

I always looked up to you, Fuck-face, (*He smiles.*)
I always knew you'd be the one
To shock half the world with your talent,
Forget-me-not when you are done.

I'll love you and lose you, so call me,
Remember your first-act, best friend,
I'll be the crutches you thankfully burn
When your mind's once more on the mend.

And if, by mishap, I should make it,
Never lose faith, my old son,
You always loved calling out 'Race me',
When you knew you'd already won.

The book falls into his lap.

It's crap, wuss.

Blackout.

The End.